"*Returning Well* sizzles with relevance and satisfies a pressing need in th
This well-paced guidebook speaks to the heart of a cross-cultural serv
With the clever use of a movie, this book is more than a 'must-read'; it is a captivating experience. As
a coach for cross-cultural sojourners, this is a practical tool I'll be recommending until I die! I wish
I'd had a copy when I returned after living more than twenty years overseas!"
  —SHERRI DODD, Founder and CEO of Advance Global Coaching

"I felt completely bewildered as I exited the airport and navigated my way through the first few days.
No, I had not just arrived in a foreign country; instead, I had come "home" to the USA. I felt far less
confidence and remarkably more anxiety than when I had arrived in the Philippines less than two
years earlier. I desperately needed a tool like *Returning Well*, and an understanding companion, to
help me integrate my experiences and thrive in this strange environment everyone referred to as my
"home." Anyone who has lived a significant amount of time in a cross-cultural environment will find
that engaging with *Returning Well* will empower them to move forward with confidence, enhanced
by the tremendous blessing of being a sojourner."
  —GLEN GIBSON, PH.D., Associate Professor of Intercultural Studies, William Jessup University

"As the president of an agency which specializes in sending cross-cultural sojourners, I regularly get
to sit with folks who, once they return home, find a level of disorientation the likes of which they've
never known. It's not uncommon for them to require months—maybe years—to readjust. Some never
completely recover. *Returning Well* could change all of that, on a massive scale. *Returning Well's* use of
specific meetings creates a guided path for returning pilgrims. And we've seen *Cast Away*, as a metaphor,
provide valuable insights for travelers in the past. What *Returning Well* does is provides a systematized
approach that can now be used at large by workers returning near or far, over time. We're deeply grateful
as an agency for this resource and can't wait to implement this in the lives of all our returning workers."
  —DOUG LUCAS, Founder and President of Team Expansion and Brigada.org

"*Returning Well* is awesome! We needed something like this when we returned in December 1985. At
that time we didn't realize the effect the transition from the field to the USA would have on our eleven-
year-old daughter, and *Returning Well's* searching look would have helped us articulate emotions and
perceptions that lay buried for years. I found the references to the movie a refreshing way of debriefing
and getting in behind surface attitudes. Bless you for this tremendous gift to people returning."
  —MARJ BOUDREAUX, PH.D., cross-cultural sojourner returned from Asia

"*Returning Well* was a great resource that helped me to actually process my experiences, which was
especially helpful when I found myself in a context that just wanted me to move on!"
  —C.D., cross-cultural sojourner who used *Returning Well* in her return from Latin America

"Because of *Returning Well*, I was able to debrief, understand how I have changed, and more fully
engage with who I am now in my primary culture."
  —B.B., cross-cultural sojourner who used *Returning Well* in her return from Latin America

"I highly recommend *Returning Well* to anyone leaving their field assignment or changing locations. Unlike other resources that explain the stress of re-entering one's home culture, *Returning Well* is designed to help the cross-cultural sojourner process the thoughts and emotions of their journey. The emphasis is on taking relevant action steps, making it more helpful. It's easy to engage with and provokes a lot of thought."

—D.H., cross-cultural sojourner who used *Returning Well* in his transition in Asia

"*Returning Well* did a great job. I needed help to go through my experiences and draw out lessons learned. *Returning Well* gave me that tool to be intentional and to move forward."

—N.B., cross-cultural sojourner who used *Returning Well* in his transition in Asia

"*Returning Well* creates a venue through which intentional reflection changes oneself. The reality is our lives are changed once we live abroad. *Returning Well* gently and at times provocatively invites us into the cross-cultural journey we've lived and stirs us to 'return well' by contemplating incredibly good questions. Don't miss this creative and effective opportunity to care for yourself and in so doing, 'return well.'"

—PAUL NIAGER, Member Care Specialist with Barnabas International

"*Returning Well* is a comprehensive resource for cross-cultural workers returning home from the field. These leaders bring a wealth of hard-won understanding and experience home with them. In an increasingly multicultural world, this wisdom could be transformational for the local fellowship, community, and the world. Yet, oftentimes the transition home is challenging and difficult, and what could be a transformational season for the cross-cultural leader as well as for the home community, sending organization, or the local fellowship is lost.

"*Returning Well* creates a bridge for the returning cross-cultural worker to journey home, not just physically, but also emotionally, culturally, relationally, and spiritually. Crafted with creativity and with great honesty, *Returning Well* invites those who are returning home to go deep in dealing with every aspect of cross-cultural transition, from leaving to readjustment. Because learning takes place best with support, the book also advocates that each worker have a companion (which may be a life coach) to walk through the transition with them and includes a section for the companion. I would highly recommend this resource to returning cross-cultural workers, to coaches and pastors, and to the local fellowship!"

—TINA STOLTZFUS HORST, Executive Director, CMI

"Re-entry is difficult, even under the best of circumstances. So, take the questions and suggestions of this guidebook seriously. If one works through each chapter thoughtfully, this guidebook will make a great difference for his or her re-entry."

—R.W., cross-cultural sojourner who used *Returning Well* in his return from Eastern Europe

"I highly recommend *Returning Well* for anyone returning from a foreign culture. *Returning Well* does an excellent job walking you through your journey of living in different cultures so that you can return well, be healthy, and be influential."

—M.C., cross-cultural sojourner who used *Returning Well* in her return from Africa

RETURNING
Well

MELISSA CHAPLIN

Published by Newton Publishers.
Requests for information should be addressed to www.NewtonPublishers.com.

ISBN 978-0-9863426-0-8

All brief quotations regarding the experience of using *Returning Well* are used with permission from individuals who engaged *Returning Well* in their re-entry and/or transition. Unless otherwise noted, all other quotations are original to the author. All sacred text references are the author's own translation.

This guidebook is in no way endorsed by or affiliated with any individuals or entities involved in the production of *Cast Away*. Copyrights and trademarks for any books, films, articles, and promotional materials are held by their respective owners.

Cover design: Tamara Dever, TLC Graphics, www.TLCGraphics.com
Interior design: Tim Murray, Paperback Design
Custom Artwork: Mecca Rutherford, Mecca Fine Art
Images: Used under license from Shutterstock.com

Most Newton Publishers books are available at special quantity discounts when purchased in bulk.
Visit www.ReturningWell.com for more information on bulk orders of this particular resource.

YOUR GUIDE TO THRIVING BACK "HOME"
AFTER SERVING CROSS-CULTURALLY

RETURNING *Well*

MELISSA CHAPLIN

NEWTON
PUBLISHERS

Contents

PART THREE: INTEGRATING

Foreword

Decades of working with cross-cultural sojourners has provided me with appreciation for the unique challenges and joys they experience as they travel our world. Just as I am honored to journey with these people as they prepare to go, I am also honored to journey with these same workers when they return. When they do return, my heart's desire in my role as a cross-cultural specialist is that these workers return well.

While resources abound for those preparing to cross into a foreign culture in terms of language learning, cultural understanding, and cultural norms, far fewer resources address the phenomenon of returning to one's home culture in terms of integrating, rather than compartmentalizing, their cross-cultural experiences.

And yet, re-entry is fraught with unimaginable challenges both glaring and subtle! In recent years, this has been recognized and has led to the development of organizational debriefing programs. I have been involved in a variety of these programs with several organizations. These specialized programs lead to health and the ability to truly return home. Unfortunately, many returning workers are not able to participate in one of these programs.

In the midst of my debriefing work, Melissa joined me as an apprentice. Quickly apparent was her talent to listen well and teach in the cross-cultural arena. During our time together, we got out our notebooks as well as the movie *Cast Away* and intently watched with our cross-cultural filters totally engaged. The impact of that experience never left Melissa.

The seeds planted in Melissa's time as an apprentice have since grown, and now my twenty years of experience debriefing, listening, and "hearing" cross-cultural workers compel me now to applaud the arrival of *Returning Well: Your Guide to Thriving Back "Home" After Serving Cross-Culturally.*

Returning Well is a guidebook you can open and easily make your own—an individually-crafted debriefing and renewal experience. You can use it with a debriefing companion, with your family, with a like-minded group, or on your own. Returning well means being able to tell not only your story, but also the story of the people you lived among, and the larger story of faith and growth that He intends.

All these years later, I am delighted to recommend this comprehensive resource totally focused on those returning from another culture. This book contains the potential to deeply impact your re-entry and renewal experience so that you can indeed return as He intended.

Donna Cole
Member Care Consultant
Board Member, Barnabas International

Introduction

You've just returned "home" after living cross-culturally. What will life be like for you in this new season? Where will you fit in? How will you think and talk about your time of living cross-culturally?

Will disillusionment steal your hope and rob you of joy? Will continually wishing you were someplace else lead you to live a life of constant frustration? Will grief overwhelm you, loneliness deplete you, or resentment isolate you? Will unanswered questions keep you awake at night?

Or will you return well?

Will you wake up looking forward to the day ahead of you? Will you live in a deep sense of peace, even when you think about what was done…and left undone? Will you not only function again but also laugh, love, and dream again? Will you enjoy being who you are and where you are? Will you find a place to belong, be known, and make a difference?

Returning Well makes a healthy re-entry possible, not by being a book to read, but by being a guidebook to engage. It is perhaps best described in two different pictures.

The first picture is actually a real story that a beloved man named John recorded hundreds of years ago about men who were invited to breakfast on a beach after facing deep grief, albeit temporary, and disrupted hopes.

The plan these men had envisioned did not turn out the way they expected and they went back "home." And while fishing back "home," they heard a strangely familiar voice, "Children, don't you have any fish?" No. "Throw your net onto the right side." John recognized Him[1] first. Peter splashed down into the water. The others followed with the boat, their hearts uplifted but now their boat heavy-laden. The only One who could revive their hopes and reset their course invited them to bring some of the fish they caught and have breakfast with Him on the beach.

He told them that what they feared was the end was really a new beginning, a beginning that was about to be born in each of them. He reinstated the one who denied him, even causing hurt as He healed. He alluded to the truth that each one now has a particular, even distinct, calling for which they are responsible to Him alone, and they are not to compare their callings. Callings are, after all, not theirs to create but theirs to accept. These renewed callings would not have been possible if they had not said yes to walking dusty roads to foreign lands with Him in the first place. But they said yes then, and so they are invited to say yes once again.

Choosing to engage *Returning Well* is choosing to "come to the beach" to have that same kind of conversation with your Creator. And for this conversation, *Returning Well* provides conversation-starters in the form of topics that follow the transition model so that you may purposefully listen for His voice on matters relevant to your experiences as a cross-cultural sojourner.

Every conversation will be different. He may lead you through deep grief and yet give healing words. He may even ask you to do hard things. He may bring clarity where you had confusion. He may bring joy and freedom in ways you never thought possible. But through it all, *Returning Well* leads you to hear from Him words of truth, understanding, wisdom, healing, and calling—words that will propel you into a revitalized future.

The second picture that describes *Returning Well* starts with a landscape. It is as if your life as a cross-cultural sojourner is a landscape abounding with treasure. Some of it is obvious, but some of it is buried beneath the surface. Part One: "Initiating," of *Returning Well* will help you discern how much of the landscape you would like to explore as well as how you want to go about your exploration. Part Two: "Inquiring," is like the map that leads you through the landscape, asking questions that help

---

[1] Note that *Returning Well* is a guidebook for people of faith serving in a wide variety of contexts. In order for it to be used in certain areas, creative synonyms have replaced the most sensitive words.

you find and polish off those precious treasures. Part Three: "Integrating," then guides you through how to use those treasures to make a real and significant difference going forward. And *Returning Well* does not expect you to go through this process entirely on your own. Instead, it equips a *Returning Well* Companion of your choosing to walk alongside you as you discern from your Creator where to explore, what to unearth, and how to put your treasures of insight to good use.

It may take some hard work. It may even take some tears. But, you will live differently because of discovering those treasures and discerning how to use them. You may be tempted to "get on with life" and step over these treasures, but in doing so, you would be missing out on some of the greatest gifts you've been given—gifts that are not only for you but also for His people.

Thank you for the honor of serving you through this guidebook as you journey through re-entry. May your heart be open to Him, may your ears hear His voice, and may you confidently walk forward from this time with Him into the future that He has for you. May your debriefing be effective and may your renewal be dynamic. And may His richest blessings be upon you as you return well!

Thriving

No eyes can see the branches that were.

But you remember them—
The heights they reached from lowly beginnings,
The vibrant greens they emanated after long, hard winters,
The shade they stretched to provide.
Perhaps that is why it feels so painful to not have them anymore.
If only they knew, you think to yourself.

And then you remember—
The leaves that were marred by pests,
The branches raw from hail,
The withering stems that went from green to gray,
Making leaves rattle empty in the wind.
And you think again—only with a different tone,
If only they knew…

These branches—the beautiful and broken—are no more.

But yet, the roots that grew and strained,
To soak up life and Living Water in new places,
To make those branches that were—
Those roots are still there, those roots are still alive,
And those roots can bring forth life again—thriving life.

Life will never look exactly the same again,
These are new shoots, after all—
A new way to be, a new way to live,
But not entirely new, because of those roots.

The roots that spread in new directions,
That stretched to savor new soils,
Yes, those same roots will send forth new shoots—
New shoots that will sprout new hope, new branches,
New expressions of life—
New shoots uniquely formed by roots that reached new lands.

New growth will take time.
It may even take seasons.
But, step by step, question by question,
Grief by grief, joy by joy,
Day by day, sunrise by sunset,
Thriving is possible—
Those roots are rooted in Love that goes deep and wide,
And they are poised to spring up new life—joyful life, full life.

So yes, thriving will look different than it ever has before.
But you can thrive again.
Are you ready to begin?

PART ONE

Initiating

Would you recommend *Returning Well* to a friend?

"Yes. I was really able to process my experience, and I know that others would feel the same way. The questions were great prompters for good searching."

"Yes. It's helpful in processing the little things which feed into the big things."

"Yes, I think it is a great resource...Returning Well is easy to engage with and helps bring out areas that need to be addressed or thought through."

"Yes, it helps you process past, current, and future experiences."

CHAPTER ONE

Your Journey

The story that you tell is the story that you believe.
And the story that you believe is the story that you begin to live.
It is important that you discover the real story,
accepting the good and the bad of where you just were and are now,
so that you can live the real story you are being given.

Choosing to engage *Returning Well* is choosing to come to the beach to have a conversation with your Creator. It is choosing to explore a landscape in order to put to good use discovered treasures of great value. And it is also choosing to embark on a journey: a journey from where you are now, having recently returned from your host culture, to a revitalized future back "home" in your primary culture. It is a journey through a debriefing that leads to renewal. Begin this journey now by understanding where you are going and customizing your plan to get there.

Prepare Your Mind and Heart for the Journey:
Recognize and Anticipate the Process to a Revitalized Future

Returning Well guides you through the process of an effective debriefing that leads to a dynamic renewal so that you may be fully released to uniquely and wholeheartedly love and serve Him in the season of life following re-entry. What is an effective debriefing and dynamic renewal?

An **effective debriefing** is reflecting on a recent season of life in order to process the specific aspects of it (events, experiences, emotions, decisions, relationships, thoughts, and actions), understand its impact personally and communally, recognize and accept its paradoxes, identify personal growth and things learned, and bring about a meaningful closure. Effective debriefing naturally leads to renewal.

"The definition of debriefing gave me a greater sense of the purpose of Returning Well."

"Working through the whole book Returning Well was definitely worth it. It all came together towards the end and resulted in me returning well."

"The movie Cast Away was a great visual aid/metaphor."

"It was nice to have a visual to attach different cultural experiences/ adjustments to."

A **dynamic renewal** is experiencing revitalized health (physical, mental, emotional, spiritual, relational, and vocational) and wholeness during the season of life following a transition. It is achieved by engaging the process of skillfully implementing action steps (that have been discerned from honing and applying debriefing insights) in such a way as to benefit others and self.

Once back "home" in your primary culture, begin your *Returning Well* journey by doing the following: Decide from the outset that a revitalized future is worth the effort, and commit to intentionally follow His leading as you engage the *Returning Well* process of a debriefing that leads to renewal through to completion. The greatest benefit from this process goes to those who stay the course.

Get a Sense of the Terrain: Watch *Cast Away*

Prepare to engage your story by watching *Cast Away*,[1] a movie that depicts transition, adjustment, and re-entry. For many, a movie is enjoyable and helps to quickly identify deeper experiences, thereby providing a more fruitful debriefing experience. Having a *Returning Well* Companion (detailed in Chapter Two) who has also watched *Cast Away* provides common reference points, further increasing the fruitfulness of your time with your companion.

You are next encouraged to watch *Cast Away* in its entirety. A *"Cast Away* Content Advisory for Faith-Based Audiences" is provided on p. 210 should you desire to be aware of scenes that may require viewer discretion. Visit www.ReturningWell.com for suggestions regarding where to buy or rent *Cast Away*. Note that, although encouraged, it is not required to watch *Cast Away* in order to benefit from *Returning Well*.

Put on Some Good Walking Shoes and Pack Your Hiking Boots: Prepare to Actively Engage

Which form(s) of your engagement proved most helpful and/or effective for you?

"Reflecting on the questions and talking them through in a one-on-one setting."

This guidebook creatively packages the significant and normal aspects of re-entry as well as the vital process of a debriefing that leads to renewal into purposeful questions. Therefore, as you invite your Creator into the process and thoughtfully engage the topics and questions in this guidebook, instead of passively reading about re-entry, you will be actively doing the necessary and beneficial, although at times challenging, work of re-entering well.

The next step in your *Returning Well* journey is to prepare to actively engage the topics in this guidebook by customizing your journey using the questions in the following section of this chapter.

---

[1] *Cast Away* is the movie where FedEx® employee Chuck Nolan (played by Tom Hanks) adjusts to living a very different life on a deserted island after a plane crash. Throughout *Returning Well*, you'll find connections to scenes from *Cast Away* in the footnotes.

Decide with Your Guide: Customize Your Journey

Returning Well is designed to be customized to fit you, your personality, and your re-entry circumstances. Prepare for a successful *Returning Well* journey by seeking wisdom from Him and determining how best to customize your engagement in the following areas.

- **What modes of transportation will I be using on this journey? (Choose Your Method(s))**

Given that every re-entry and returning person is unique, engage the questions in this guidebook in ways that are most effective for you, taking into consideration your personality and re-entry circumstances. For instance, you could reflect on the questions through journaling, drawing, painting, or talking with a friend. Alternatively, you could reflect while riding a bike, walking, or something else altogether. The important thing is to take time to intentionally engage the questions and glean insights in ways that best fit you.

The next step is to ask Him for wisdom, and then choose which method(s) of engagement best fit you, your personality, and your re-entry circumstances. Jot down the methods you plan to use in the space provided to the right.

- **What is important for me to see on this journey? (Determine Your Time Period and Cultures)**

The next step in customizing your *Returning Well* journey is to determine the time period you will be debriefing in order to reach renewal. To do this, choose to address either the entire time you spent in your most recent host culture (i.e., the culture in which you were recently serving and have recently left) or, if different, your most recent season of service in that host culture.

For example, if you served for ten years in your host culture (perhaps with a few short stints back to your "home"/primary culture), you may decide to debrief that entire ten-year season. Alternatively, if you had a two-year home assignment in the middle of that ten-year period, you may decide only to debrief the most recent four-year season in your host culture.

Take a moment to ask Him which period of time in your most recent host culture He would like you to debrief in order to reach renewal, and jot it down to the right.

Next, determine which culture(s) you will consider to be your primary culture(s) based on your chosen time period. This guidebook is written with the assumption that, for most sojourners, you have recently returned to your primary culture (otherwise known as your passport or home culture, or the culture to which you have the greatest personal affinity). But, for those with varied cultural experiences, this

"I think the personal reflection was most meaningful. I did a lot of processing, and that is what I remember and take forward the most."

"I spent most of my time individually, and it was most effective when I wrote down my thoughts."

"It was most effective when I took time to intentionally recall various events and circumstances."

My Method(s)

My Time Period

My Primary Culture(s)

My Host Culture

assumption may be too simplistic, and in that case *Returning Well* is adaptable to fit your situation.

In all situations, to determine your primary cultures, consider the following:

- First, bring to mind your chosen time period in your host culture that you are debriefing. In what culture did you live before you started this season of service? That is the primary culture from which you moved to serve in your host culture.

- Then, consider the culture to which you have recently moved. This is the primary culture to which you have transitioned, or in most cases, returned. For many sojourners, these cultures are the same. But, if they are different for you, as you go through *Returning Well* you will be able to determine which primary culture each topic refers to by the context of the questions.

Before continuing, jot down to the left which cultures you will consider to be your primary culture(s) and host culture as you use this guidebook.

What are my primary cultures if I have served in multiple host cultures?
▶ If you have served in multiple host cultures, as you determine your primary cultures, consider the following example. Julie grew up in the USA. As an adult, she left the USA and served several sequential seasons of cross-cultural service, going to Italy, then to Spain, then to Honduras, and then to Venezuela before returning to the USA. The best season for her to debrief first is the one in her most recent host culture: Venezuela. The primary culture she was in prior to moving to Venezuela was Honduras, and her primary culture to which she returned is the USA. After she completes the *Returning Well* process related to Venezuela, she will then consider if and how she wants to use the *Returning Well* process to debrief her previous seasons of cross-cultural service (i.e., Honduras, Spain, and Italy).

"Engaging Returning Well over a period of time helped me to practically and emotionally process while I transitioned. I was able to let things sink in and truly get perspective in my heart."

- **How long do I want my journey to last? (Pick Your Pace)**

So that you may reap the full benefits that come from completing this re-entry process, *Returning Well* plots out three paces of engagement: a six-week pace, a three-month pace, and a six-month pace. Depending on the intensity of the experiences you are debriefing, your chosen method of engagement, and your re-entry circumstances, your next step is to ask for His wisdom, and then determine if you would like to engage *Returning Well* over a period of six weeks, three months, six months, or a custom time period. Jot down your chosen pace on the following page. Once you decide your pace, the "Get the Most" pages at the beginning of Part Two:

"Inquiring" and Part Three: "Integrating" will help you discern how many topics or chapters to engage during an average day or week to stay on track.

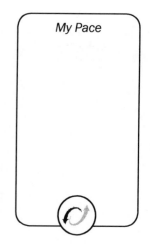

My Pace

What does it mean when *Returning Well* says... ▶

"...this recent season"?	The season of service that you have just lived in your host culture; i.e., the season that you are debriefing.
"...this season"?	This time of re-entry which is a time of transition lasting until you reach a new normal in your next season of life.
"...the next season of life" or "coming season"?	This is the season of life after re-entry; i.e., once you have reached a new normal and a dynamic renewal.

- **Which route do I want to take? (Discern Your Approach)**

As you engage each chapter in Part Two: "Inquiring," note that others have found *Returning Well* helpful to engage in one of three approaches:

Highlight Approach: Approach each chapter by only engaging the core topics. Cumulatively, these core topics create an essentials-only route and are further described on p. 8–9 as well as demarcated by this icon ↻ in the "Topics in This Chapter" at the start of each chapter.

Scenic Approach: Consider engaging every topic in the order presented.

Blended Approach: Approach each chapter by first engaging the core topics and then, according to your available time and energy, by briefly considering any other topics in the chapter that you feel led to respond to before moving to the next chapter.

To determine your approach, take into consideration your chosen method, the season you are seeking to debrief and reach renewal on, and your re-entry circumstances. Consider the following examples:

Linda is a loving mom with two children, each in their own major transition with one child getting married and the other starting college. She

What helped you to get the most out of your *Returning Well* engagement?

"Having some of the questions marked as most important (the core topics) helped me focus my thoughts, particularly at times when I felt like my time was limited."

chose only to consider the core topics in each chapter during her morning exercise routine and gave herself freedom to pass by the rest.

Robert is a teacher passionate about learning and writing who lived with a host family for eight years in a culture very different from his primary culture. Upon his return, he had a thirty-minute bus ride every morning and thoroughly enjoyed using that time to journal his responses to every applicable topic straight through.

Paul is a personable big-picture thinker. He enjoyed glancing at all of the topics in a chapter straight through in one sitting and then deciding which he felt most led to engage. He reflected on these questions and talked through them with others as he went about daily life. Once he got clarity, he would then briefly jot down his thoughts.

Julie was not sure how much time she would have, but she knew which topics she most needed to focus on given her cross-cultural experiences. She chose the blended approach, giving her attention first to the core topics and then to any other topics that resonated with her felt needs as she had time and energy. Once she got clarity, she drew sketches that captured her insights.

My Approach

For your engagement to be effective, it is imperative that you choose an approach that is fitting to you. Also, always give yourself freedom to skip any questions that you do not sense Him leading you to respond to, that do not apply to you, or that do not interest you. Different questions will be more valuable to you during different seasons of debriefing, so be okay with not responding to all the questions.

After completing this chapter and Chapter Two, your next (and very significant) step in your *Returning Well* journey is to actively engage the topics and questions in Part Two: "Inquiring" that are appropriate for your specific re-entry journey using a fitting approach. Take a moment to jot down your chosen approach (highlight, scenic, or blended) to the left.

What is a core topic? ▶ All three approaches make use of core topics. In order for a topic to be deemed a core topic, it had to meet the following four criteria:

- The topic is applicable to the vast majority of cross-cultural sojourners.
- The topic is a fundamental component of most healthy debriefings.
- The topic engages deeper personal, relational, or spiritual experiences.
- The topic has direct, often immediate, application to moving forward in re-entry.

The core topic route was developed to enable an essentials-only path through debriefing that leads to renewal, in awareness of significant constraints that apply to some sojourners in re-entry. However, non-core topics still generally meet two or three of the criteria just listed, and for most sojourners will also be highly valuable to engage.

How do I actually determine which topics or questions to engage? ▶ First, choose your approach (highlight, scenic, or blended) as it will determine which topics you will even begin to consider. With your approach decided, following are suggestions for choosing which particular topics and questions to engage:

- First and foremost, maintain a conversational yet humble posture. Ask Him for wisdom, and be sensitive to His leading with every question.
- Ask yourself, "Which questions would I want someone to ask me?" and then engage those.
- Follow your interest, and respond to questions that hold intrigue for you.
- Purposely engage questions that relate to your significant experiences. For instance, reflect on the language-learning topics if you went about language learning during the season of service that you are addressing.

- **Who do I want at my side? (Find a *Returning Well* Companion)**

Because your *Returning Well* journey will be abundantly more beneficial if you engage a skilled and trusted *Returning Well* Companion with whom you can process your reflections, Chapter Two and the "Serving as a *Returning Well* Companion" article (pp. 203–209) provides you and your companion(s) with the resources needed for such an endeavor to be successful.

Next, after reading Chapter Two, ask for His provision of a *Returning Well* Companion, and then enlist a companion (or a group of companions) to walk alongside you on your re-entry journey according to your chosen pace. Once secured, arrange for him or her to obtain a copy of the article, "Serving as a *Returning Well* Companion." (You have permission to copy or share electronically pp. 203–209 of this guidebook for this purpose or use the code SERVING when prompted at www. ReturningWell.com/Resources for an electronic version.) Note that you do not need to wait until you have a *Returning Well* Companion to engage the topics in Part Two: "Inquiring." It is usually best to begin engaging these topics as soon as you are ready. Take a moment to jot down to the right some names of people who you would enjoy inviting to be your companion.

"I liked that I had time to reflect and [talk with my Creator regarding] the questions in Returning Well. But then it was encouraging to talk through the questions with my companion and get a chance to express my discoveries to another person."

My Potential Companions

Finish Strong: Live Out Renewal

**What about
Returning Well was
most powerful and
effective for you?**

*"The application
chapter—pulling it all
together was helpful."*

- **Live Renewed by Applying Significant Insights**

Insights without application stop short of their full potential. Thus, after completing Part Two: "Inquiring" to your satisfaction, use Chapter Twenty-One to hone your debriefing insights into action steps. Then, live out renewal by implementing those action steps in the next season of life.

- **Make a Difference with Your Words by Crafting Your Communications**

**How did *Returning
Well* make a
difference in your re-
entry?**

*"Returning Well
has helped me in
communicating
with others."*

A common re-adjustment challenge is explaining your cross-cultural life and experiences to those not personally familiar with your host culture. And given that sharing your story is immensely valuable, not only for your thriving in the next season but also for the Kingdom, Chapter Twenty-Two will give you tools to help you put your cross-cultural service, transition, and insights into words. If you are expected, or are planning, to share about your cross-cultural life and experiences immediately upon re-entry, consider reading Chapter Twenty-Two as you prepare to do so, and then engage it again after completing Chapter Twenty-One.

Additional Frequently Asked Questions

For whom and when is *Returning Well* most useful? ▶ This guidebook may benefit any person of faith in re-entry, and it is most useful for those who have served at least one year in a host culture, are returning to spend at least one year in their "home" or primary culture, and are engaging *Returning Well* during the first year following their departure from their host culture.

I am currently receiving professional counseling/psychological services. Can I still use *Returning Well*? ▶ It is not uncommon for cross-cultural sojourners to experience psychological difficulties—and even related physical difficulties—during their re-entry adjustment, and *Returning Well* does not seek to replace professional services pertaining to such difficulties. In such situations, it is usually best to consult your professional counselor or psychologist regarding the advisability of using *Returning Well* in your situation.

CHAPTER TWO

Your Returning Well Companion

What was most enjoyable about engaging *Returning Well* for you?

"I loved having someone who didn't experience life with me overseas and who I could share with because she committed to being my companion."

One of the most valuable gifts you can give yourself for your *Returning Well* journey is seeking out a *Returning Well* Companion. A *Returning Well* Companion is someone

- you trust and with whom you feel safe,
- who can and will keep confidences,
- who is skilled at listening well,
- who is genuinely interested in your story and cares about you as a person,
- who is likely to be comfortable with and accepting of a wide range of emotions, and
- with whom you can share most all aspects (the fun and the difficult) of your cross-cultural life and subsequent re-entry.

One very consistent theme discovered as others used the preliminary version of this guidebook was the value of a well-chosen companion. The majority of those with the most successful outcomes from *Returning Well* all had trusted companions skilled in empathetic listening. And most everyone who did not have a companion thought their experience would have been better had they found one. Being able to choose topics from *Returning Well* and then verbally process them with a skillful companion greatly enhances the journey to a revitalized future. Whether it is a friend, family member, laity at a fellowship, professional life coach, counselor, or member care practitioner, please give yourself this valuable gift, and find at least one *Returning Well* Companion.

"I came back from my time in Cameroon worried about how I was going to adjust and if I'd feel like a stranger in my own culture. Going through Returning Well and having a companion helped me to see what challenges and blessings I had in Africa and how they affected my views and relationships in my home culture."

Asking a Companion to Join You

When you ask a companion to join you in this endeavor, consider the following:

- Overtly request that your companion spend a specific amount of time helping you process your experiences. Consider asking for six meetings that are about two hours each. The optimal spacing of these meetings depends on your chosen pace for engaging *Returning Well*.

If your chosen pace to engage *Returning Well* is over	Your optimal meeting schedule would be
six weeks	once a week
three months	twice a month
six months	once a month
a custom time period	tailored to your chosen pace

Following is a suggested plan for your meetings:

- During Meeting One, build rapport and process your initial transition experiences.

- During Meeting **2**, share from Chapter Three through Chapter Eight.

- During Meeting **3**, share from Chapter Nine through Chapter Fourteen.

- During Meeting **4**, share from Chapter Fifteen through Chapter Nineteen.

- During Meeting **5**, share from Chapter Twenty through Chapter Twenty-One.

- During Meeting **6**, share from Chapter Twenty-Two and bring closure to your time together by celebrating key insights gained and solidifying next steps.

- Clearly articulate who you would like to have join you at these meetings, whether it is just your companion or if you are inviting others.

- Request that your companion read the article titled, "Serving as a *Returning Well* Companion" located on pp. 203–209 (p. 9 has options for obtaining a copy of the article). This article equips your companion with a general understanding of transition, provides an outline of the meeting plan, suggests specific questions for your companion to ask you at each meeting, and encourages him or her to watch *Cast Away*. When sharing this article with him or her, mention that you can provide a "*Cast Away* Content Advisory for Faith-Based Audiences" if desired. (You have permission to copy or share electronically p. 210 if needed.)

- And don't forget that you may begin engaging the questions in Part Two: "Inquiring" on your own prior to having your companion in place.

Frequently Asked Questions

 What if I can't find a companion who lives near me? ▶ If your companion of choice does not live near to you, give yourself the freedom to consider meeting with your companion by phone or video/electronic means.

 Can my spouse be my companion? ▶ You are welcome to have your spouse serve as your companion provided he or she desires to do so. At the same time, you will also likely benefit from having an additional companion who is not your spouse—but that person should be someone who is also trusted by your spouse, considering the personal nature of many of the topics covered.

 Should my companion be from my host or primary culture? ▶ In most situations, you will find the greatest benefit in having a companion from your primary culture, i.e., the culture to which you have recently returned.

 Can I have more than one companion? ▶ Yes, you may find it beneficial to have more than one *Returning Well* Companion.

"I thought it [Cast Away] was a tangible example of what one experiences in a new host culture and upon their return to their home culture…not only for those who had the experience but also as something that could be referenced to help others understand what it's like to re-integrate into a culture/society that others expect you to claim, know, and relate to."

PART TWO

Inquiring

A glimpse of what is ahead...

*"I'm more aware of who I am now and how I've changed.
I was able to debrief and more fully engage with who I am
now in my primary culture."*

*"It helped me process and think through my experiences
and gain new perspectives."*

*"It helped me reflect on my frustration, and instead of blaming
someone, I just took it as a normal process of adaptation
to my new context."*

*"Because I can tell the growth and changes my experience has
made in me, I know how to be prepared for my next stage."*

*"It gave me confidence to move on knowing I am not leaving
things from the past undealt with."*

Get the Most out of Part Two: "Inquiring"

Optimize your *Returning Well* journey through Part Two: "Inquiring" by engaging the topics in the following ways:

Engage according to your method (such as journaling, reflecting, drawing, talking with others, etc.).

Engage with clarity on the season of service you are addressing.

Engage with clarity on your host and primary culture(s) (based on the season of service you are addressing).

Engage at your chosen pace using your chosen approach.

If you are using the	and the <u>highlight</u> or <u>blended</u> approach, consider on average	and the <u>scenic</u> approach, consider on average
six-week pace,	three or four core topics each day.	one chapter each day.
three-month pace,	one or two core topics each day or about eleven core topics each week.	four topics each day or three chapters each week.
six-month pace,	one core topic each day or six core topics each week.	two topics each day.

Engage by maintaining a conversational yet humble posture. Ask Him for wisdom and sensitivity to His leading with every topic and question.

Engage with freedom to skip any topics or questions that you do not sense Him leading you to respond to, that do not apply to you, or that do not interest you.

Further enhance your engagement of Part Two: "Inquiring" by meeting with your companion. Following is the suggested plan for your meetings:

- During Meeting **2**, share from Chapter Three through Chapter Eight.

- During Meeting **3**, share from Chapter Nine through Chapter Fourteen.

- During Meeting **4**, share from Chapter Fifteen through Chapter Nineteen.

get the most

Are you ready? Part Two: "Inquiring" begins the process of an effective debriefing that leads to a dynamic renewal. Through engaging these topics and questions in conversation with your Creator, you will be DOING the beneficial work of returning well!

CHAPTER THREE

Departure and Initial Transition

Which questions were most memorable and/or helpful?

"Chapter Three through Chapter Ten and the 'discovery' of how I have been changed from when I arrived to when I left India. It was good to be reminded of where I came from/who I was when I arrived and then who I was when I left—how I had learned to appreciate things that in the beginning were difficult. So for me, it was the whole 'journey' through those chapters."

"I think the first two chapters of Part Two and the first few questions were memorable because it was going back in time so far. It was like thinking about a whole different person I was at that time. Since leaving, I had thought a lot about the end, about regrets or things I never finished but wanted to. But going back to the beginning felt really free, almost like watching the beginning of a movie I've seen a lot of times before, knowing how it will end and what's coming next but just enjoying the simplicity of it all."

Topics in This Chapter

- Reflections from *Cast Away*
- World-View Prior to Departure to Host Culture
- Departing Your Primary-Culture Relationships
- ↻ Calling

- Valuing Transition Wisdom
- ↻ In the Throes of Transition
- Primary-Culture Assets No Longer Valuable
- Grieving Transition Losses
- ↻ Glean and Go Forward

Take a moment to ask Him for wisdom as you begin your *Returning Well* journey.

Reflections from *Cast Away*

What scenes are most poignant to you? What makes each poignant?

What parts of the movie most closely resemble your transition experiences?

World-View Prior to Departure to Host Culture

In order to begin understanding how this recent season of service influenced you, think back to the season before you left for your host culture. What was your lifestyle like?

What were your highest priorities? What did you most value?

What caused you stress?[1]

---

[1] Chuck is driven by the clock, impatient, and a perfectionist.

How did others know you?

Departing Your Primary-Culture Relationships

What significant relationships did you have prior to your departure to your host culture?[2] How did the way that you departed affect these relationships?

What expectations did others in your primary culture have of you as you departed to your host culture? In what ways did these expectations influence your departure?

What have you found to be some of the best ways to honor others while still caring for yourself as you make transitions that take you a far distance away from them?

Calling

What calling were you responding to when you left for this recent season of service?

→

---

[2] Chuck is called into work and gives Kelly gifts prior to departure.

CORE TOPIC

Living your calling is at times a lot like skydiving: It can be exhilarating yet intimidating, some people think you are crazy

(continued next page)

For meeting

(continued from previous)
*while others wish they
had the guts to do
what you are doing,
and while you would
really like to have
a graceful landing,
many times you are
just hoping that you
make it through alive.*

How, if at all, did others try to dissuade you? What were the effects of their attempts?

When, if ever, did you doubt your call or your ability to fulfill it? How were you able to work through these doubts?

Which aspects of this calling, if any, still apply?

Valuing Transition Wisdom

What did others tell you about your upcoming transition before you experienced it?

What value did these comments hold for you?[3]

---

[3] After awaking to a storm, Chuck ignores advice to sit and goes to the bathroom.

In the Throes of Transition

What was the initial stage of your transition to your host culture like? How did it compare to your expectations?[4]

What habits, mindsets, or resources most helped you through this initial stage of transition (such as practical transition skills, relationships, attitudes of the heart or mind, specific Truths, etc.)? What made each helpful?

Which of these, or particular aspects of these, might be helpful to you now as you transition back to your primary culture? In what ways might they be helpful?

CORE TOPIC

If cultures were like friends, then one key to transitioning well is realizing that some-times the best way to get reacquainted with an old friend is a lot like getting to know a new friend.

Primary-Culture Assets No Longer Valuable

What values, knowledge, skills, and belongings that you relied on in your primary culture did you no longer find useful in your host culture?[5] How did you discover that they were no longer useful?

→

---

[4] Chuck fights to survive in the water following the explosion.
[5] Chuck realizes that some things he relied on daily, like his watch, are not useful on the island.

For meeting

What was it like for you to no longer need these things that were part of your primary-culture life?

What, if anything, did you find useful in their place?

Grieving Transition Losses

What losses from your transition to your host culture were most difficult for you? How did you grieve these losses?

How did the way that you grieved affect your transition to your host culture?

What, if anything, would you want to do differently as you grieve losses in this transition back to your primary culture?

Glean and Go Forward

Once you have completed this chapter to your satisfaction, take a moment to review your responses, taking note of the following:

- Identify one valuable item, i.e., something that stands out to you, holds meaning for you, has a strong emotional impact on you, or you sense Him bringing to your attention. Record it on p. 170.

- Next, identify anything you sense Him leading you to know or do based on this chapter. Record it on p. 172.

- Finally, identify which questions you would like to explore and insights you would like to share with your companion. Star them or jot them to the right.

CORE TOPIC

Questions & Insights

"[It was] effective to record valuable items as I went along, so they were there ready to be pondered at the end and used as a place to search for themes and patterns."

By the way, before you continue on, how did this chapter go for you? Are you satisfied with your pace, approach, and method? If so, keep on keeping on! If not, give yourself permission to adjust. You are on an important journey — renewal awaits — so be sure to engage Returning Well in such a way as to enjoy the process!

For meeting

  3 4 5 6

CHAPTER FOUR

A Dream Come True?

What was most enjoyable about engaging *Returning Well* for you?

"I enjoyed having specific questions to help me process."

"I'm glad I was able to process the many random ideas in my head and feel some sense of progress."

What about *Returning Well* was most powerful and effective for you?

"I think the part about traumatic experiences was great to include. I think remembering how I handled difficulties was important and helped me cope with the re-adjustment and reverse culture-shock."

Topics in This Chapter

- Seeking Help
- Adjusting to New Sounds and Events
- Facing Fear
- Ineffectiveness and Mistakes
- Adjustments in Daily Life

- First Explorations and Initial Impressions
- Traumatic Experiences
- Grieving Death
- Glean and Go Forward

Take a moment to ask Him for wisdom as you continue your *Returning Well* journey.

Seeking Help

In what ways did you seek out help when you arrived in your host culture?[1] What were the effects of seeking out help in these ways?

How are you seeking out help now as you re-enter and transition again? Which of these have been most helpful to you?

Adjusting to New Sounds and Events

What was your initial reaction to any new sounds or events that you experienced when you first arrived in your host culture?[2] How did you adjust to them?

What sounds or events have most stood out to you in your season of re-entry? What has experiencing these been like for you?

---

[1] Chuck creates help messages on the beach.
[2] Strange thuds disturb Chuck. He later discovers that these noises are falling coconuts.

Facing Fear

What were you afraid of in your host culture?

How did experiencing these fears impact you?

In what ways were you able to overcome these fears? What helped you do so?

What fears are you facing in re-entry?

How do you want to respond to these fears?

CORE TOPIC

Walking free from fear is like turning on the light after groping in the darkness: You can see more clearly, step more confidently, respond more wisely, and breathe more easily.

For meeting

CORE TOPIC

Being ineffective or making a cultural mistake can be like trying to learn how to ballroom dance and painfully tromping on the feet of the one person you are trying to impress: It is an acute opportunity for both growth and grace.

Ineffectiveness and Mistakes

What are some ways you attempted to accomplish new tasks in your host culture that were initially ineffective?[3] What gave you motivation to try again?

How did you most commonly respond to cultural mistakes that you made while living in your host culture? How did this response influence your cultural adjustment?

What was different about the times you responded well to your ineffectiveness and mistakes?

Which of these ways of responding would most effectively help you to handle well any ineffectiveness or mistakes during re-entry? How might they be helpful?

[3] Chuck struggles to open a coconut and start a fire.

Adjustments in Daily Life

What aspects of your life that were easy in your primary culture became exceedingly *more* difficult and/or time-consuming in your host culture?[4] Which aspects of your life that were burdensome in your primary culture became significantly *less* difficult and/or time consuming in your host culture?

More difficult and/or time-consuming in host culture	*Less difficult and/or time-consuming in host culture*

What new tools, skills, or habits did you discover and employ in order to adapt to these changes in daily living in your host culture?

What did the process of adjustment to these new ways of life look like for you?

---

[4] Chuck painfully toils at starting a fire.

First Explorations and Initial Impressions

What are some of your most poignant memories from your first explorations of your host culture?[5] What did you see, hear, and smell?

What emotions did you have?

What were your initial impressions?

In what ways, if any, did these impressions change by the time you left to return to your primary culture?

What have been your initial impressions of your primary culture in this season of re-entry?

---

[5] Chuck explores the island and surveys it from the top of a peak.

Traumatic Experiences

What traumatic experiences impacted you while you were in your host culture?[6] In what ways did they impact you?

In what ways have you experienced physical, emotional, and spiritual healing from these traumatic events? What facilitated this healing for you?

Physical healing

Emotional healing

Spiritual healing

Of the traumatic events you experienced, which, if any, continue to bring you distress? What would help bring resolution to these events that still cause you distress?

---

[6] Chuck turns over the body of one of his colleagues floating in the water.

For meeting
2 3 4 5 6

Grieving Death

Consider any encounters with death that you had while living in your host culture. How did you grieve?

Now consider how those in your host culture responded to death. How did their responses influence your grief, if at all?

What has been most helpful to you as you have experienced grief?

CORE TOPIC	Glean and Go Forward
Questions & Insights	Once you have completed this chapter to your satisfaction, take a moment to review your responses, taking note of the following: • Identify one valuable item, i.e., something that stands out to you, holds meaning for you, has a strong emotional impact on you, or you sense Him bringing to your attention. Record it on p. 170. • Next, identify anything you sense Him leading you to know or do based on this chapter. Record it on p. 172. • Finally, identify which questions you would like to explore and insights you would like to share with your companion. Star them or jot them to the left.

CHAPTER FIVE

Accepting and Adapting

What about *Returning Well* was most powerful and effective for you?

"It was very helpful to me to have specific questions to work through, rather than just trying to reflect in hazy generalities, or go around in circles on the same two or three topics. It gave a great, rounded perspective."

"Active engagement rather than passive receiving of information. Capturing insights and thinking through how to apply them into new situations."

What most surprised you about *Returning Well*?

"I was surprised at the depth of identifying and capturing parts of the cross-cultural experience."

Topics in This Chapter

- **Finding Food**
- **Cultural Food**
- **From Escaping to Admiring**
- **Relying on Resources**

- *C* **Expectations**
- *C* **Frustration and Anger**
- *C* **Glean and Go Forward**

Take a moment
to ask Him for wisdom
as you continue your
Returning Well journey.

Finding Food

What most surprised you as you initially went about obtaining food in your host culture?[1]

What did you enjoy about where, how, or from whom you obtained food in your host culture?

How did you manage any cultural challenges you encountered in securing food?

Cultural Food

What role did food play in your host-culture's customs and values? How did these food customs and values affect you?

What host-culture foods did you most enjoy? Which did you least enjoy?[2]

Most enjoy	Least enjoy

---

[1] Failing at capturing fish and refusing to eat raw crab, Chuck struggles to find food.
[2] Chuck's diet on the island primarily consists of coconut, crab, and fish.

What foods or dishes from your host culture do you hope to continue to enjoy in your primary culture?

From Escaping to Admiring

Consider your adjustment to your host culture. How, if ever, did you try to escape the culture?[3] What do you think your "escaping" looked like to others?

What did it take for you to try new things that were uncomfortable for you to do?

What unexpected gifts did you find when you stepped outside of your comfort zone?

What aided you in becoming more accepting of the parts of your host culture that originally challenged you the most?

What did you come to most admire and appreciate about your host culture?

---

[3] Chuck fails at fleeing the island. Seeking shelter from a storm, he finds water in a cave.

For meeting

2 3 4 5 6

Relying on Resources

Which resources from your primary culture did you initially rely on to survive, even thrive, in your host culture?[4] As time passed, how did the importance of these resources change for you?

Which resources from your host culture are you now relying on during this season of re-entry into your primary culture?

CORE TOPIC

Expectations are like rocks. Some can be unnoticeable and simply part of the landscape. Others can be helpful, providing walking paths and places to sit and rest. But others can be heavy, creating a load impossible to carry or even being impediments to moving forward. It takes wisdom, courage, and intentionality to transform that which is impossible to carry and an impediment

(continued next page)

Expectations

What were the most prominent expectations that you had during this recent season of life in your host culture in the following areas?

Yourself

Your host culture

Your life in general

---

[4] Chuck's flashlight dies after he falls asleep with it on.

Your role(s)

(continued from previous) *into something that is helpful and a place of rest.*

Your friendships

Your family

Your team/colleagues

Your sending group(s)

What would be accomplished and/or your length of service

Any other pertinent areas of life

→

For meeting

 4 5

Now go back and underline the expectations that were met. Circle the expectations that were never realized.

What were the effects of any unrealized expectations?

What wisdom could you glean from these experiences in expectations that would be helpful to take forward into the next season of life?

CORE TOPIC

Frustration and anger can be excellent teachers, revealing deeply held values, expectations, and attitudes of the heart. Ignoring them is passing up

(continued next page)

Frustration and Anger

What most frustrated and angered you in your host culture?[5]

---

[5] Chuck's failed attempts at starting a fire leave him injured, angry, and trying again.

How did you respond, both inwardly and outwardly, to these things that caused you frustration and anger?

Inwardly

Outwardly

What did you learn about yourself through these experiences of frustration and anger?

For what, if anything, do you experience guilt or regret as you recall instances of expressing your frustration and anger? If needed, what are the next steps toward healing?

In what ways and to what extent were you able to handle well these things that caused you frustration and anger?

→

(continued from previous) *significant opportunities for self-awareness, growth, and at times even repentance.*

For meeting

What has frustrated and angered you in re-entry?

How might you apply your awareness from the previous questions in this topic to the things that are frustrating and angering you in re-entry?

CORE TOPIC

Questions & Insights

Glean and Go Forward

Once you have completed this chapter to your satisfaction, take a moment to review your responses, taking note of the following:

- Identify one valuable item, i.e., something that stands out to you, holds meaning for you, has a strong emotional impact on you, or you sense Him bringing to your attention. Record it on p. 170.

- Next, identify anything you sense Him leading you to know or do based on this chapter. Record it on p. 172.

- Finally, identify which questions you would like to explore and insights you would like to share with your companion. Star them or jot them to the left.

CHAPTER SIX

Relationships and Communication

What were some of your most poignant take-aways from engaging *Returning Well*?

"I realized how my slow development of community overseas was a great hindrance in adjustment there—took about five years to really have solid community. It was fear of sharing weakness that kept me back from the community I needed then. This is a huge lesson to be applied now, and I am actively developing community just one year in."

Which questions were most memorable and/or helpful?

"Very good questions on processing your experience in the host culture (friendships, stresses, smells, etc.). Helped me think back very specifically to the things I saw and did in Mexico."

Topics in This Chapter

- Loneliness
- Friendships
- Belonging
- Conflict in Relationships
- Forgiveness

- Reconciliation
- Communication Styles
- Language Learning
- Language Ability
- Glean and Go Forward

Take a moment to ask Him for wisdom as you continue your *Returning Well* journey.

Loneliness

When, if ever, did you experience loneliness in your host culture? How do you think others perceived your loneliness?

What helped to alleviate your loneliness?

Circle any of these, or aspects of these, that might help you to alleviate any loneliness you are now experiencing in re-entry.

Friendships

How did you develop friendships in your host culture?[1] What influence did your host culture have on the process of developing friendships?

Which friendships, including with both nationals and expatriates, were most meaningful to you? What made each meaningful?

---

[1] Chuck makes a face on the volleyball, and it becomes his new friend, Wilson.

Belonging

Where or with whom did you come to feel that you belonged—that you were known and accepted? What contributed to you developing that sense of belonging?

Where or with whom might you now find belonging?

Conflict in Relationships

Think about some of the most challenging conflicts you encountered with both nationals and expatriates in your host culture. What effects did these conflicts have on you?

In what ways did you contribute to these conflicts?

What influence did any cultural differences have on these conflicts?

→

CORE TOPIC

Experiencing a challenging conflict in a cross-cultural setting can be like being in a car accident: Once it has happened you feel shaky, your vision is blurred, your heart is racing, and you're wondering what happened to cause it. You hesitate getting into a car again until you've taken time to heal and your trust in the driver (possibly yourself) has been restored.

For meeting

How did you personally grow from these conflicts?

What did you learn from experiencing these conflicts in your host culture that you could apply to any conflicts you are encountering in re-entry?

If harboring bitterness, holding a grudge, or only seeing another's flaws is the infection, then forgiveness is the antiseptic.

Forgiveness

In what ways, if any, did withholding forgiveness impact your life in your host culture?

How is withholding forgiveness impacting you now, if at all?

Who, if anyone, do you need to forgive? What might help you to do so?

For what, if anything, and from whom do you need to ask for forgiveness? How might you go about doing so?

Reconciliation

How did you pursue reconciliation in your relationships while living in your host culture? What did you gain from these pursuits?

Which of your relationships, if any, currently need reconciliation? What steps could you take toward the reconciliation of these relationships?

As you take steps toward reconciliation, what might it look like for you to practically reject bitterness and instead act with compassion, kindness, gentleness, and respect?

In the relationships where you have attempted reconciliation and it has not been successful, what will help, or has helped, you to reach a place of peace?

CORE TOPIC

Reconciliation is like a dance—sometimes beautiful and flowing, sometimes choppy and jerky—and getting started requires one humble initiation and two willing partners.

For meeting

Communication Styles

From your perspective, what three words best describe your host-culture's style of communication? How did each of these influence your style of communication?

As you re-enter, what are you noticing anew as to how those in your primary culture communicate?

Language Learning

How did your language-learning experiences differ from your expectations?

What aspects of language learning challenged you the most? What made these aspects challenging?

What did you discover was the most effective way for you to go about language learning?

If you desire to continue using or learning your host-culture language(s) in this coming season, how might you go about doing so?

Language Ability

What is your internal response when you think about how well you were able to communicate in your host-culture's language(s)?

What two words would you use to describe your ability to communicate in your host-culture's language(s)? What about your language ability makes these two words seem appropriate?

In what ways did your ability to communicate in your host-culture's language(s) influence how you viewed yourself?

Given your previous responses, what do you want to celebrate or need to resolve, if anything, in the area of language ability to move forward toward a healthy re-entry?

Celebrate	*Resolve*

CORE TOPIC

Questions & Insights

"I liked the 'Glean and Go Forward' at the end of each chapter. It was helpful to bring out valuable things."

Glean and Go Forward

Once you have completed this chapter to your satisfaction, take a moment to review your responses, taking note of the following:

- Identify one valuable item, i.e., something that stands out to you, holds meaning for you, has a strong emotional impact on you, or you sense Him bringing to your attention. Record it on p. 170.

- Next, identify anything you sense Him leading you to know or do based on this chapter. Record it on p. 172.

- Finally, identify which questions you would like to explore and insights you would like to share with your companion. Star them or jot them to the left.

How are you doing? If your pace, approach, and method are working well for you, then keep on keeping on—and blessings as you do so!

However, if you are starting to feel bogged down, this is a good time to consider altering your approach (perhaps becoming more selective in what topics you engage), adjusting your method (perhaps engaging the questions in a different way or in a different setting), or modifying your pace (perhaps giving yourself more or less time).

It is critical that you continue moving through the gleaning you are doing in Part Two: "Inquiring" so that you can fully engage the process of reaching renewal in Part Three: "Integrating."

CHAPTER SEVEN

Cross-Cultural Living

"I know that I have said it a lot, but there were many times I thought I had dealt with every aspect, and then something else would be sparked by a question."

Which questions were most memorable and/or helpful?

"Questions that focused on how experiences shaped me personally and changed me. They were meaningful because they helped me think about what the past sixteen years of my life have been about."

Topics in This Chapter

- Celebrating Success
- Host-Culture Political and Social Climates
- Host-Culture Brokenness
- Influencing Others

- Your Ethnicity and Nationality
- Attention and Privacy
- Safety and Danger
- Glean and Go Forward

Take a moment
to ask Him for wisdom as you continue your *Returning Well* journey.

CORE TOPIC

Celebrating a success is like reaching a breath-taking vista after an arduous hike: It is an opportunity for your eyes to remind your legs that you are getting somewhere and that it's worth it to keep going.

Celebrating Success

How did you react when you accomplished what was once a seemingly impossible feat in your host culture?[1]

Of all the cross-cultural accomplishments you experienced, which ones brought you the deepest sense of personal satisfaction? How did you or will you celebrate these successes?

Host-Culture Political and Social Climates

Consider the predominant characteristics of the political and social climates of your host culture. How did these political and social climates affect you personally?

How did these political and social climates influence your work and its reception in your host culture?

What do you mean by "political and social climates"? ▶ A political climate is the population's cumulative sentiments of those currently in power and of how power is gained. A social climate is the social and civil functioning as well as the prevailing psychological state of a society.

---

[1] Chuck celebrates starting a fire with joy, pride, and a bonfire.

Host-Culture Brokenness

What brokenness did you observe in your host culture? How did it affect you?

CORE TOPIC

Cultural brokenness is like a chronic illness: It is an ever-present source of groaning for healing and an opportunity for a miracle cure.

Which responses to this brokenness were most redemptive?

What are your greatest hopes for how this brokenness may be healed?

Take a moment to lift these hopes up to Him.

If you were to encounter such brokenness again (in your primary culture or elsewhere), how do you think He would desire you to respond?

Influencing Others

Who did you most desire to reach out to and influence while in your host culture? What wisdom did you glean from your efforts at reaching out and seeking to influence them?

$\rightarrow$

For meeting

Who might you now desire to reach out to and influence in your primary culture? How might the wisdom you gleaned cross-culturally guide you as you consider reaching out in your primary culture?

Your Ethnicity and Nationality

How did those in your host culture typically react to your ethnicity and nationality?

In what ways were your ethnicity and nationality assets in your host culture? How were you able to utilize these assets?

In what ways were your ethnicity and nationality hindrances in your host culture? To what extent were you able to overcome these hindrances? How did you go about doing so?

Attention and Privacy

Think about any instances where you felt as though you were on display in your host culture, i.e., instances when you were given special attention or when you lacked privacy. What were these experiences like for you?

What did you find to be effective strategies for handling these experiences?

What, if anything, do you miss about this kind of attention?

Safety and Danger

In what ways did you feel safe in your host culture?

What dangers or threats to your safety, both tangible and spiritual, did you experience in your host culture? What were the effects of these on you?

What healing (emotional, physical, and spiritual) do you still desire, if any, from these experiences? How might you go about seeking this healing?

→

CORE TOPIC

It took courage to go to parts unknown.

When darkness came, it took courage to believe.

Shining His light on those memories will take courage once again...

But, doing so may be what is used to further illuminate the way forward.

For meeting

When did you most obviously experience His protection when faced with these dangers and threats to your safety?

What wisdom did you or could you gain from dealing with these dangers and threats to your safety?

What dangers and threats to your safety, both tangible and spiritual, are you experiencing in re-entry? How might you apply the wisdom you gleaned from experiencing dangers and threats cross-culturally to these dangers and threats you are now experiencing?

CORE TOPIC

Questions & Insights

Glean and Go Forward

Once you have completed this chapter to your satisfaction, take a moment to review your responses, taking note of the following:

- Identify one valuable item, i.e., something that stands out to you, holds meaning for you, has a strong emotional impact on you, or you sense Him bringing to your attention. Record it on p. 170.

- Next, identify anything you sense Him leading you to know or do based on this chapter. Record it on p. 172.

- Finally, identify which questions you would like to explore and insights you would like to share with your companion. Star them or jot them to the left.

CHAPTER EIGHT

Sojourner Truths

What were some of your most poignant take-aways from engaging *Returning Well*?

"Highlighted the sheer number of transitions and losses in our life over the sixteen years. I have been shaped by loss and grief."

What was most enjoyable about engaging *Returning Well* for you?

"Seeing the breakdown of my experience in terms of topics and understanding their implications to my experience and relationships."

Topics in This Chapter

- Moving Residences
- Fluctuations in Community
- Feeling at "Home"
- Homesickness
- Relationships with Those Far Away

- Stints in Your Primary Culture
- Partnership Development
- Wealth, Spending, and Finances
- Available Services
- Glean and Go Forward

Take a moment to ask Him for wisdom as you continue your *Returning Well* journey.

Different residences are like the different seasons: Some provide more opportunity for growth than others.

Moving Residences

Consider the places that you lived from the moment you left your primary-culture residence prior to departure until now.[1] What were the living conditions and arrangements like in each place? What influence did each place have on you?

Residence and living conditions/ arrangements	*Influence on you*

Which residence was most refreshing? What made it refreshing?

---
[1] Chuck moves from his tent to a more stable home in the cave.

Which residence was most draining? What made it draining?

Given your previous responses, what considerations might you take into account as you settle into another residence?

Fluctuations in Community

Consider the fluctuations of friends and colleagues you experienced while in your host culture. In general, what impact did these fluctuations have on you?

Which fluctuations were most significant to you? What made them significant?

In what ways do you think your own departure to your primary culture impacted others in your host-culture community?

→

Fluctuating community is like a revolving door of constant hellos and goodbyes: At first the novelty can be intriguing, but after a few revolutions you're feeling dizzy and perhaps a little nauseous, and you realize that enjoying this kind of "community" requires being unusually intentional.

For meeting

Given your responses on this topic, if and when you experience fluctuations in community in the future, what would you want to do again? What would you want to do differently?

Do again	Do differently

Feeling at "Home"

What items did you use to adorn your host-culture residence(s)? What significance did these items hold for you?

When, if ever, did your host-culture residence(s) begin to feel like "home"?

When, if ever, did your host culture itself begin to feel like "home"?

What helped to make your host culture, including your residence(s), feel like "home"?

Circle any of these items from the previous questions in this topic that could help make your primary culture, including your residence, feel like "home."

Homesickness

When, if ever, did you feel homesick? What most often prompted your feelings of homesickness?

What did you learn about yourself through these experiences of homesickness?

In what ways are you now homesick for your host culture?

Relationships with Those Far Away

Which relationships with those living a far distance from you (such as friends and family) had the most significant impact on you, for the better or the worse, while you served in your host culture?[2] What was the impact of each of these relationships on you?

What concerns did you have for your friends and family who were physically distant from you while you served in your host culture? How did these concerns affect your life in your host culture?

$\rightarrow$

---

[2] Chuck admires a picture of Kelly that he drew in the cave.

For meeting

2 3 4 5 6

What advice would you give to others on handling relationships with those far away while adjusting to and living in another culture?

Circle any aspects of this advice that might be relevant for you as you handle relationships with those far away while adjusting to and living in your primary culture.

Stints in Your Primary Culture

What two words best describe any stints you had in your primary culture during this recent season? What about these stints makes these two words appropriate?

What have you discovered to be some best practices for making these stints enjoyable and beneficial?

When did you wish that you could have traveled to your primary culture and could not? How were you able to make peace with not being able to travel at that time?

(?) **What do you mean by "stints in your primary culture"?** ▶ A primary-culture stint is any period of time that you spent in your primary culture during the season of host-culture service that you are debriefing. A stint can last from a few days to several months and include what many refer to as a home visit, home assignment, sabbatical, or furlough.

Partnership Development

What did you find helpful about the way you approached partnership development, both while you were living in your primary culture and in your host culture?

Which of your personal skills, gifts, and strengths did you find most beneficial in partnership development? In what ways were they beneficial?

What influence has doing partnership development had on your relationships and faith walk?

Relationships

Faith walk

If partnership development will continue in the next season of your life, what, if anything, do you want to change about how you go about doing it? If partnership development is coming to a close for you, how might you show appreciation to your partners and bring closure to your season of partnership?

 What is partnership development? ▶ Partnership development is sometimes referred to as fundraising, fund development, itineration, or support raising.

Wealth acts like clothing:

Too little and you're underdressed, embarrassed, and maybe even feeling shame.

Too much and you're overdressed, feeling awkward, out of place, and maybe even guilty.

Just enough and you're appropriately dressed, feeling confident, relaxed, and thankful.

Wealth, Spending, and Finances

From your perspective, how did your host culture define wealth?

What effect did this definition have on how you viewed wealth? What effect did it have on your financial decisions?

How you viewed wealth

Your financial decisions

While living in your host culture, what other events influenced your values related to wealth and spending?

What have been the effects of any financial challenges that you faced while living in your host culture and during re-entry?

What beneficial financial habits do you desire to continue in the next season? What changes, if any, do you sense Him desiring you to make in how you handle your finances in the next season?

Beneficial habits to continue	Changes to make

Available Services

What services from your primary culture, if any, did you lack in your host culture? How did you accommodate the lack of these services?[3]

What services, if any, did you enjoy having in your host culture that you do not have in your primary culture? What is helping you to adjust to these losses?

---

[3] Lacking a dentist, Chuck fixes his tooth himself.

CORE TOPIC

Questions & Insights

Glean and Go Forward

Once you have completed this chapter to your satisfaction, take a moment to review your responses, taking note of the following:

- Identify one valuable item, i.e., something that stands out to you, holds meaning for you, has a strong emotional impact on you, or you sense Him bringing to your attention. Record it on p. 170.

- Next, identify anything you sense Him leading you to know or do based on this chapter. Record it on p. 172.

- Finally, identify which questions you would like to explore and insights you would like to share with your companion. Star them or jot them to the left.

CHAPTER NINE

Proficiency and Completion

What about *Returning Well* was most powerful and effective for you?

"Really seeing how my experience overseas changed me through small things I learned to do was so amazing. I would write about my skills I learned and be fascinated that that small thing changed who I am."

What helped you to get the most out of your *Returning Well* engagement?

"The questions were also so specific that it was a great tool for thinking more intensively than I otherwise would have about my experience."

Topics in This Chapter

- ↻ **Areas of Mastery**
- • **Physical Adaptations**
- • **Pace of Life**
- ↻ **Departure Preparations**
- • **Rhythms of Life**
- • **Host-Culture Traditions and Celebrations**
- • **Gift Giving**
- • **Valuing Time**
- ↻ **Glean and Go Forward**

Take a moment to ask Him for wisdom as you continue your *Returning Well* journey.

CORE TOPIC

Like the rings of growth on a tree are your areas of mastery—markers showing seasons of growth which provide strength, stature, and stability for the next growing season.

Areas of Mastery

In general, how did your host-culture competency develop?

What areas of struggle in your host culture eventually became areas of mastery?[1]

Of the skills you learned in your host culture, which are most helpful to you as you re-enter your primary culture?

Physical Adaptations

What effect did the climate of your host culture have on you?

How did your physical body adapt to living in your host culture?[2]

---

[1] Four years later, Chuck fishes with impeccable precision.
[2] Chuck's body has slimmed, and his clothes have become primitive.

How did your clothing preferences, habits, and styles shift to adapt to your host culture?

What did the process of adjusting to your host-culture's climate as well as its clothing preferences, habits, and styles look like for you?

What has most surprised you about your primary-culture's climate as well as its clothing preferences, habits, and styles upon your return? In what ways have you already begun re-adapting to these aspects of your primary culture? What has that been like for you?

Pace of Life

What three words best describe the pace of life you had in your host culture? What about that pace of life makes these three words appropriate descriptors?

What pace of life do you think He desires for you in this next season of life? What are some ways you might go about adjusting to or maintaining this pace?

CORE TOPIC

Whether your departure was planned or surprising, desired or dreaded, the reasons for your departure can be like the spices in a dish: They are often invisible yet they poignantly change your experience, sometimes making it sweet and enjoyable, other times sour, and sometimes even bitter enough to give a terrible aftertaste that leaves your senses dulled until your palette is cleansed.

Departure Preparations

What were the events and circumstances that led up to the decision to leave your host culture?

When did you physically begin packing to leave your host culture?[3] How did you decide what you would take with you?

When did you begin emotionally packing to leave your host culture? What did your emotional packing entail?

How did the reason for your departure as well as your emotional packing impact your departure?

How has the desire to leave your host culture, or lack thereof, affected your re-entry?

---

[3] Chuck prepares to leave by gathering valuable things from the island.

Rhythms of Life

What was the yearly rhythm of life in your host culture?[4] What did you most enjoy about this rhythm?

In the coming year, what do you anticipate will be the major differences in the rhythm of life in your primary culture? What, if anything, are you most looking forward to in these differences?

Host-Culture Traditions and Celebrations

Which host-culture traditions and celebrations held the most meaning for you? What made them meaningful to you?

Which of these, if any, do you hope to continue observing in some way in this next season of life? How might you go about doing so?

---

[4] Chuck notes the tides and breezes as he decides his departure schedule.

For meeting
2 **3** 4 5 6

Gift Giving

Consider the expectations and customs your host culture had for giving gifts. What did the process of you adjusting to these gift-giving expectations and customs look like?

How have your host-culture's gift-giving habits influenced your own values regarding gift giving?

Valuing Time

Several continua for how a person values time exist. They include, but are not limited to, the following:

- Being punctual, goal-directed, and proactive with time versus being flexible, spontaneous, and responsive.
- Arriving at an event at the stated start time (or slightly earlier) versus changing one's current focus at the stated start time in order to begin preparing for and traveling to the event.
- Seeing the completion of an event being based on a preset time (e.g., the event ends at 5:30) versus the particular objectives of the event being accomplished.
- Enjoying completing a task versus developing a relationship.
- Cherishing special dates of the past versus treasuring the events of the present.
- Saving time through being orderly, planned, and efficient versus accommodating the day's events through being relaxed, accepting, and patient.
- Directing one's own time versus allowing another to direct one's time.
- Focusing on one single priority until its completion versus willingly accepting interruptions.

These are just a few examples of how one can value time. Nuances and variations between the options listed above add to the myriad ways a person and culture may value time.

What time values did you hold prior to transitioning to your host culture?[5]

What were the major time values of your host culture? How did these values influence the way you valued time?

How do you value time now? What influence are these time values having on your re-entry?

Glean and Go Forward

Once you have completed this chapter to your satisfaction, take a moment to review your responses, taking note of the following:

- Identify one valuable item, i.e., something that stands out to you, holds meaning for you, has a strong emotional impact on you, or you sense Him bringing to your attention. Record it on p. 170.

- Next, identify anything you sense Him leading you to know or do based on this chapter. Record it on p. 172.

- Finally, identify which questions you would like to explore and insights you would like to share with your companion. Star them or jot them to the right.

CORE TOPIC

Questions & Insights

---

[5] Chuck recalls his lecture to the Russian employees and grasps the irony his words now hold.

For meeting

CHAPTER TEN

Appreciating Adversity

"Returning Well helped me face the difficulties of returning home. Remembering how I handled difficult situations in my host culture helped me through the transition and reverse culture-shock that I was experiencing in my home culture. It also encouraged me to persevere and seek additional guidance."

Which questions were most memorable and/or helpful?

"Dealing with stress and different ways your body reacts to stress. I didn't realize how stressed I was and how it was affecting me on a physical level."

Topics in This Chapter

- Managing Stressors
- Facing Personal Wellness Challenges
- Accepting Mercy and Forgiveness

- Dreams and Goals
- Giving Thanks in Adversity
- Glean and Go Forward

Take a moment to ask Him for wisdom as you continue your *Returning Well* journey.

CORE TOPIC

Like forming a precious pearl through a painful irritation is discerning a healthy habit for managing stressors: Treasure it dearly.

Managing Stressors

Cross-cultural sojourners encounter significant amounts of stress in the course of their transitions and seasons of life that they live cross-culturally. It is important to understand more fully the significant stressors you experienced as well as what you can gain from each. In the following areas of stress common to cross-cultural sojourners, list the most significant stressor(s) you experienced while living in your host culture as well as what you were doing differently when you handled each stressor well.

Supply Stress (i.e., stress related to lack of a particular resource such as funds, time, energy, rest, staff, community, medical services, utilities, etc.)[1]

My most significant stressor(s)	*What I was doing when I handled each well*

Occupational Stress (i.e., stress related to your particular role(s) as you served cross-culturally)

My most significant stressor(s)	*What I was doing when I handled each well*

Leadership Stress (i.e., stress related to working under the authority of another as well as stress related to having authority over another)

My most significant stressor(s)	*What I was doing when I handled each well*

---

[1] Chuck is overwhelmed at how little time he has to accomplish his pre-departure tasks.

Organizational Stress (i.e., stress related to the policies, practices, and procedures of the organization(s) with which you worked and/or in which you operated)

My most significant stressor(s)	*What I was doing when I handled each well*

Disposition Stress (i.e., stress related to being placed in a position where you were required to act in a way contrary to your natural tendencies and inclinations)

My most significant stressor(s)	*What I was doing when I handled each well*

Relational Stress (i.e., stress related to relationships with your colleagues, other expatriates, nationals, family, friends, your spouse, your child(ren), etc.)

My most significant stressor(s)	*What I was doing when I handled each well*

Cultural Stress (i.e., stress related to the habits, customs, beliefs, practices, and values of your host culture)

My most significant stressor(s)	*What I was doing when I handled each well*

→

For meeting

 2 **3** 4 5 6

Crisis Stress (i.e., stress related to any shocking or disconcerting incident, accident, situation, or disaster)

My most significant stressor(s)	What I was doing when I handled each well

Physical Stress (i.e., stress related to your health such as challenges with nutrition, sleep, energy, weight loss or gain, injury, illness, chronic pain, or the physical climate)

My most significant stressor(s)	What I was doing when I handled each well

Emotional Stress (i.e., stress related to your internal responses to life and events)

My most significant stressor(s)	What I was doing when I handled each well

Spiritual Stress (i.e., stress related to your faith walk as well as experiences with the spiritual realm)

My most significant stressor(s)	What I was doing when I handled each well

As you consider your previous responses, what are some of the main things that you were doing differently when you handled your stressors well?

What are seven significant stressors as you re-enter?

1.

2.

3.

4.

5.

6.

7.

How might you apply what you have learned from handling stressors cross-culturally to these re-entry stressors?

For meeting

CORE TOPIC

Like dirty laundry, we'd rather hide our personal wellness challenges, although airing them out in the right environment might just be the best way to stop the stink.

Facing Personal Wellness Challenges

What, if any, personal wellness challenges did you face? (These may include such things as anxiety, burnout, depression, trouble concentrating, chronic illness or fatigue, atypical indecisiveness, insomnia or other sleep disturbances, addictive behavior, uncontrollable anger or extreme irritability, unusual forgetfulness or confusion, considerations of suicide, sexual impurity, and the like.)[2]

What effect did your most significant personal wellness challenges have on you, your relationships, your faith walk, and your work?

You

Your relationships

Your faith walk

Your work

What Truth do you need to remember and believe when considering these challenges?

[2] Chuck retrieves the rope he used when considering suicide.

Which of your responses to these challenges were most beneficial?

What work, if any, remains for you in resolving these challenges? What makes such work important to complete? Who could you enlist to help and/or support you as you seek resolution?

Accepting Mercy and Forgiveness

Review your responses to the previous topic. Of the personal wellness challenges you listed, for which ones, if any, do you still need to accept His mercy and forgiveness? What will help you to do so?

For which ones, if any, do you still need to be merciful toward and forgiving of yourself? What will help you to do so?

For meeting

2 **3** 4 5 6

Dreams and Goals

Reflect on the major dreams, goals, and undertakings you pursued during this recent season of life in your host culture. How might you celebrate those that were realized?

What, if anything, did you pour much of your energy into only to see it thwarted, unsuccessful, or never realized? What was that experience like for you?

How, if at all, were you able to work through any hurt that was caused by that experience? What hurts, if any, do you still need to work through?

In what ways did this situation refine you? How might this refinement be valuable to you in the coming season?

Giving Thanks in Adversity

As you consider the stressors and challenges that you faced cross-culturally, for what are you thankful?

What would be a refreshing way to express your thankfulness to your Creator?

CORE TOPIC

Saying thank you, over time, can transform some of the deepest anguish and most difficult hardship into profound, exquisite, and transcendent joy, even in the midst of pain.

Glean and Go Forward

Once you have completed this chapter to your satisfaction, take a moment to review your responses, taking note of the following:

- Identify one valuable item, i.e., something that stands out to you, holds meaning for you, has a strong emotional impact on you, or you sense Him bringing to your attention. Record it on p. 171.

- Next, identify anything you sense Him leading you to know or do based on this chapter. Record it on p. 172.

- Finally, identify which questions you would like to explore and insights you would like to share with your companion. Star them or jot them to the right.

CORE TOPIC

Questions & Insights

For meeting

CHAPTER ELEVEN

Leaving

How did *Returning Well* make a difference in your re-entry?

"It was helpful in that it caused me to consider aspects of the transition more than I probably would have otherwise. It was good to slow down and reflect."

"It helped me process my re-adjustment experience and helped guide me to reflect on things that were at times painful to think about."

"This guidebook was a great chance for me to search myself and identify how my experience changed me."

Topics in This Chapter

- Leaving and Saying Goodbye
- Releasing Responsibilities
- Departing Your Host Culture
- Reflecting on Your Departure
- Host-Culture Friendships
- Glean and Go Forward

Take a moment to ask Him for wisdom as you continue your *Returning Well* journey.

Leaving and Saying Goodbye

Which people, places, things (including animals), and aspects of culture were most important to you in your host culture? What made each important? How did the way that you said goodbye (or the lack thereof) most predominately affect you, and if applicable, your relationship(s)?

People, places, things, and aspects of culture—including what made each important	How the way you said goodbye (or the lack thereof) most predominantly affected you, and where applicable, your relationship(s)
People	
Places	

Things

Aspects of culture

How does your faith influence the way you think about having left these people, places, things, and aspects of culture?

To which people, places, things, and aspects of culture did you want to say goodbye but did not have an opportunity to do so? How could you say goodbye to them now?

For meeting

2 3 4 5 6

Releasing Responsibilities

Which of your host-culture responsibilities were most difficult for you to release? What made these particular responsibilities difficult for you to let go?

What, if anything, is left outstanding for you in the releasing of these responsibilities, both in practice and in your heart? What might be some beneficial next steps in this process?

What sorts of responsibilities would you find enjoyable in this next season?

CORE TOPIC

Leaving your host culture can feel like a roller-coaster ride: It starts with growing anticipation that changes into incredible speed,

(continued next page)

Departing Your Host Culture

What were the final hours in your host culture like? What emotions did you experience?[1]

[1] Chuck fears departure the night before. The next day, he celebrates overcoming the waves before feeling sadness as he looks back.

What was most delightful about leaving your host culture?

(continued from previous) *adrenaline-producing turns, surprising stomach-churning twists, and then what may feel like an abrupt end to an "exciting" life.*

What was most painful about leaving your host culture?

If you were to capture both the delightful and the painful into one picture, what would that picture look like?

What value might this picture hold for you as you re-enter?

Reflecting on Your Departure

As you reflect on your departure, for what are you thankful?

CORE TOPIC

Reflecting on your departure is like taking time to taste your food, learning how to repeat the delicious and, when possible, avoid the unpalatable.

→

For meeting

What are a few special memories that you will cherish from your departure in the days to come?

If given another departure opportunity, what would you want to be sure to do again? What would you want to do differently?

Do again	Do differently

Host-Culture Friendships

What do you miss most about your host-culture friendships?[2]

---

[2] Despite Chuck's best efforts, Wilson floats away.

What memories do you cherish as you think about these friendships?

If possible, in what ways do you want to nurture these friendships going forward?

Glean and Go Forward

Once you have completed this chapter to your satisfaction, take a moment to review your responses, taking note of the following:

- Identify one valuable item, i.e., something that stands out to you, holds meaning for you, has a strong emotional impact on you, or you sense Him bringing to your attention. Record it on p. 171.

- Next, identify anything you sense Him leading you to know or do based on this chapter. Record it on p. 172.

- Finally, identify which questions you would like to explore and insights you would like to share with your companion. Star them or jot them to the right.

CORE TOPIC

Questions & Insights

For meeting

   5 6

CHAPTER TWELVE

Back "Home"?

"Returning Well helped me remember that I wasn't the only one going through re-entry shock, and the questions helped me process when I couldn't always get to the bottom of my feelings by myself. I think it has and will continue to help me reflect on and integrate my foreign experience into my next stages of life."

What most surprised you about *Returning Well*?

"The many, many issues that would not be dealt with if a person assumes that everything will naturally 'return to normal' once he or she gets back home. The worker has changed, and the home culture is always changing. The book helps us see the various areas that need to be addressed."

Topics in This Chapter

- **Changed Preferences**
- **Cultural-Resource Person**
- ↻ **"Home"?**
- ↻ **Beginning to Re-Adjust**

- ↻ **Re-Entry Workload and Priorities**
- **Re-Entry Overwhelm**
- ↻ **Glean and Go Forward**

Take a moment
to ask Him for wisdom
as you continue your
Returning Well journey.

Changed Preferences

Which preferences of yours, if any, most dramatically changed after living in your host culture? When did you realize that these preferences changed?[1]

How have those who knew you before you left for your host culture responded to your changed preferences?

How can you help others get reacquainted with the "new" you?

Cultural-Resource Person

Who are some people in your primary culture that might serve as cultural-resource persons for you in this season of re-entry? In what ways might they help you?[2] What questions do you have for them?

---

[1] Stan assumes Chuck's preferences have remained unchanged. Chuck thinks he will like ice, yet he quickly spits it out.
[2] Stan explains the welcome ceremony plan and expectations.

What other forms of support might help you to achieve a healthy re-entry? How might you go about receiving this support?

What is a cultural-resource person? ▶ A cultural-resource person is someone who can be relied on to skillfully and gladly help you adjust to your primary culture by answering your primary-culture questions (such as, "What does it mean when someone says..." or "What are these new gadgets at the store?") as well as connecting you with primary-culture resources (such as ethnic grocery stores, nearest recreation areas, medical care, etc.).

"Home"?

What expectations did you have for how you would be welcomed back to your primary culture?[3] How did your actual return compare to these expectations?

How have you responded, both inwardly and outwardly, when others say "welcome home"?

Inwardly

Outwardly

→

[3] The plane lands, and a crowd welcomes Chuck home.

CORE TOPIC

An innocent, "Welcome home!" can be the cause of an internal tailspin: Where is home? And why do I feel like I am not there? But, I am there. And then when I do get "there," why is it that I am missing where I just was? How is it that I can call so many places "home," and yet wherever I go, I still feel out of place— like a foreigner with a familiar face?

But once you rightly maneuver the controls, smooth

(continued next page)

For meeting

(continued from previous) *flying will begin to calm the spin just endured, and you'll know how to better respond the next time around.*

CORE TOPIC

Returning to your primary culture can be like wearing someone else's shoes: Even though they're your size, your feet don't fill the grooves like they are supposed to, and the awkward sensations seem constant. Your feet ache for the day when the shoes truly feel like they are your own.[4]

What is home to you?

Beginning to Re-Adjust

Which aspects of your primary culture have been most delightful to you upon your return? Which aspects have been most disconcerting?

Delightful	*Disconcerting*

What insights do your responses reveal as to how this recent season in your host culture has influenced you?

[4] Adapted from A.W., written during his re-entry from Asia.

Re-Entry Workload and Priorities

What is your workload like, both personal and professional, during this season of re-entry?[5]

Six months from now, what will you be glad that you prioritized during this season of re-entry?

What habits will help you positively address your most important re-entry priorities in light of your current workload?

Determining what matters most in re-entry is like emerging from a dense fog: It is a relief to finally see a way forward.

Re-Entry Overwhelm

What is most overwhelming to you right now in this re-entry?

---

[5] At the welcome party, Chuck is briefed on his many re-entry tasks that start early the next day.

$\rightarrow$

For meeting

When you've been overwhelmed in the past, what has most effectively brought you refreshment, reduced your sense of being overwhelmed, and at the same time honored Him and others?

In what ways might you be able to implement that strategy in this current season?

CORE TOPIC

Questions & Insights

Glean and Go Forward

Once you have completed this chapter to your satisfaction, take a moment to review your responses, taking note of the following:

- Identify one valuable item, i.e., something that stands out to you, holds meaning for you, has a strong emotional impact on you, or you sense Him bringing to your attention. Record it on p. 171.

- Next, identify anything you sense Him leading you to know or do based on this chapter. Record it on p. 173.

- Finally, identify which questions you would like to explore and insights you would like to share with your companion. Star them or jot them to the left.

CHAPTER THIRTEEN

Re-Integrating

What was most enjoyable about *Returning Well* for you?

"The encouragement from remembering what I experienced and what He has done."

"I was most engaged by chapters thirteen through sixteen because I've been struggling with re-adjustment and closure these past few months, so I felt they were helpful."

Which questions were most memorable and/or helpful?

"'Faith Encounters' helped me see how He was at work. These are easier to see as one looks back over several years."

Topics in This Chapter

- Large-Group Gatherings
- Appreciating and Transitioning Fellowships
- ↻ Re-Integrating into a Primary-Culture Fellowship

- ↻ Spiritual Life
- ↻ Faith Encounters
- ↻ Being Transformed by His Truth
- Relational Courtesies
- ↻ Glean and Go Forward

Take a moment to ask Him for wisdom as you continue your *Returning Well* journey.

Large-Group Gatherings

What have you most and least looked forward to about large-group gatherings or events (such as attending a welcome party or sharing at a fellowship) upon your return?

Most looked forward to	*Least looked forward to*

When large-group gatherings have gone well for you in the past, what were you doing that contributed to them going well? How might you go about implementing these actions at future large-group gatherings?

What expectations do you think these groups have of you?

Appreciating and Transitioning Fellowships

What did you appreciate about the fellowship(s) that you were a part of in your host culture?

In what ways did your host-culture fellowship(s) most significantly influence you?

What has been challenging about returning to fellowship(s) in your primary culture? What has been a blessing to you in returning to fellowship(s) in your primary culture?

Has been challenging	*Has been a blessing*

 What is a fellowship? ▶ A fellowship is a group that comes together around a common faith, purpose, and/or set of beliefs.

Re-Integrating into a Primary-Culture Fellowship

What are some ways in which you would enjoy getting involved in the life of a local fellowship?

→

CORE TOPIC

Re-integrating into a primary-culture fellowship is like being a piece of a puzzle and finding the place where you fit again: It may take a few tries to find the place you fit best, but

(continued next page)

For meeting

(continued from previous)
it's worth the effort—you were made to be connected and are an integral piece to completing the picture.

What might hinder you from re-integrating well into the life of a local fellowship? What could help you to overcome these hindrances?

How might your cross-cultural service enhance how you are involved in the building-up of a local fellowship?

In the event that you have more than one option when it comes to joining a fellowship, what are some of your highest values that would help you determine which one to join?

CORE TOPIC

Growing spiritually is like adding several logs to a campfire: Doing so enables the fire to keep giving warmth and light to all those around.

Spiritual Life

What three words best describe the predominant spiritual attitudes and practices of those in your host culture, both expatriates and nationals? How did these attitudes and practices affect your spiritual life?

How did serving in your host culture provide you with opportunities for spiritual growth that you otherwise would not have likely had in your primary culture?

In what ways did you grow in your love for others while living in your host culture?

In what ways did you most powerfully experience His love for you while living in your host culture?

What habits did you find most spiritually nourishing while in your host culture? Which of these would help you to transition well?

In what ways are you feeling led to grow in how you express your spiritual life in this next season?

For meeting

2 3 4 5 6

Faith Encounters

What experiences in your host culture most tested your faith?

What faith experiences from this recent season stand out to you as particularly remarkable?

During what situations did you perceive that He most extraordinarily acted?

What did you witness Him do in and through the lives of the people you were seeking to serve?

How did these faith encounters from the previous questions most distinctly affect your faith walk? How did they most distinctly influence your view of Him?

Faith walk

View of Him

In what ways could your testimony of these faith encounters encourage others?

Being Transformed by His Truth

During this recent season in your host culture, which passages from His Book were most meaningful to your faith walk? How did your Creator use these passages to transform you?

What words of Truth is He drawing to your attention in re-entry? How is He using them in your life?

For meeting

Relational Courtesies

What are some of the most striking relational courtesy differences (such as greetings, goodbyes, visits, etc.) between your host culture and primary culture?[1]

Which host-culture courtesies do you miss? What do you miss about them?

Which primary-culture relational courtesies have been the most awkward to re-adjust to in your transition? What might help you re-adjust well to these?

CORE TOPIC

Questions & Insights

Glean and Go Forward

Once you have completed this chapter to your satisfaction, take a moment to review your responses, taking note of the following:

- Identify one valuable item, i.e., something that stands out to you, holds meaning for you, has a strong emotional impact on you, or you sense Him bringing to your attention. Record it on p. 171.

- Next, identify anything you sense Him leading you to know or do based on this chapter. Record it on p. 173.

- Finally, identify which questions you would like to explore and insights you would like to share with your companion. Star them or jot them to the left.

[1] As they leave the party, some colleagues wave while others give Chuck a hug.

CHAPTER FOURTEEN

Recognizing Change

What about *Returning Well* was most powerful and effective for you?

"The topic of 'Grieving Unfulfilled Longings' was powerful because I think the grieving period has lasted longer than I expected, and it was helpful to remember that it's part of the process."

How did *Returning Well* make a difference in your re-entry?

"Since we moved back to the place we were before China, it was very easy to fall back into a routine and almost forget that we lived overseas. This guidebook helped me reconcile that things have changed, and I am better for it."

Topics in This Chapter

- Your Role Identity
- Different Kinds of Abundance
- Witnessing Wastefulness
- Re-Adjustments in Ease
- Inferiority and Conceit

- Adopted Host-Culture Habits
- Grieving Unfulfilled Longings
- Heart Posture
- Glean and Go Forward

Take a moment to ask Him for wisdom as you continue your *Returning Well* journey.

Changes in your role identity can be like becoming a piano virtuoso and then moving back to a place where there are no pianos.

Your Role Identity

How did others come to know you in your host culture? In what did you become an expert that is not valued, understood, or recognized in your primary culture?

How do others know you now?

What things have those in your primary culture said that show a lack of understanding of your life in your host culture and who you have become?[1] How have you responded to these experiences?

What do you think might be His greater purposes behind this role identity change for you?

[1] One colleague implies that Chuck needs to work on his fishing skills.

Different Kinds of Abundance

What kinds of abundance did you encounter in your host culture? What kinds of abundance are you encountering in your primary culture during re-entry?[2]

Abundance in host culture	*Abundance in primary culture*

What has been your response to these experiences of abundance?

Witnessing Wastefulness

In general, how did your host culture define wastefulness? How did this definition influence what you viewed as being wasteful?

From your perspective, in what ways was your host culture wasteful? In what ways do you now perceive that your primary culture is wasteful?[3]

Wastefulness in host culture	*Wastefulness in primary culture*

$\rightarrow$

---

[2] Alone, Chuck surveys the table covered with large amounts of many different kinds of food.
[3] Chuck notices many plates with food left uneaten.

How would you now describe your values regarding wastefulness?

Re-Adjustments in Ease

What things that were difficult to do in your host culture are you now able to do with relative ease?[4] What things that were easy to do in your host culture are now more difficult to do in your primary culture?

Difficult to do in host culture, now easy	*Easy to do in host culture, now difficult*

What have these transitions in ease been like for you?

Review your responses to, "Adjustments in Daily Life" on p. 31. What wisdom can you glean from those responses, if any, that would assist you in making these re-adjustments in ease?

---

[4] Chuck picks up a crab leg and looks at it. He picks up a lighter and lights it.

Inferiority and Conceit

When are you most tempted to feel inferior during re-entry? What could practically help you to overcome these temptations?

When are you most tempted to be conceited during re-entry? What could practically help you to overcome these temptations?

Adopted Host-Culture Habits

What habits did you adopt from your host culture that you now continue in your primary culture?[5]

How might some of these habits seem awkward or unusual to those in your primary culture?

Circle any of the habits from the previous questions in this topic that you would like to intentionally continue and integrate into the next season of life.

[5] Chuck finds it more comfortable to sleep on the floor than in the soft bed.

For meeting

CORE TOPIC

*Grieving unfulfilled
longings can be
a lot like climbing
a mountain and
experiencing a loss
of oxygen: It may not
be a loss that you
can see, but it is still
real, noticeable, and
life-altering, and it
makes every step up
the mountain difficult
until you take the
time necessary to
adjust to and accept
your new reality.*

Grieving Unfulfilled Longings

What things did you long to return to in your primary culture only to realize now that they no longer exist or have changed dramatically?[6]

What other losses from this recent transition have been most difficult for you?

What will help you grieve well and say goodbye to these things?

How will you know when you have grieved well?

---

[6] As Chuck lies on the floor, he clicks the light on and off of Kelly's picture.

Heart Posture

If you were to describe the current attitude of your heart in one word, what would that word be? What about your heart's posture makes this word seem appropriate?

Ask Him, "What is the one word by which You would desire my heart attitude to be described?" Write that word below.

If these two words from the previous questions are different, what might the journey from the word you listed to the word you received from Him look like?

Glean and Go Forward

Once you have completed this chapter to your satisfaction, take a moment to review your responses, taking note of the following:

- Identify one valuable item, i.e., something that stands out to you, holds meaning for you, has a strong emotional impact on you, or you sense Him bringing to your attention. Record it on p. 171.

- Next, identify anything you sense Him leading you to know or do based on this chapter. Record it on p. 173.

- Finally, identify which questions you would like to explore and insights you would like to share with your companion. Star them or jot them to the right.

CORE TOPIC

Questions & Insights

For meeting

CHAPTER FIFTEEN

Re-Connecting

Which questions were most memorable and/or helpful?

"The questions dealing with the adjustments of coming back and how some relationships were different. It opened my eyes to how my relationships had changed with certain people that I couldn't pinpoint before."

What was most enjoyable about engaging *Returning Well* for you?

"Going through the whole book—if I had stopped before the 'applying' section, it would not have been as helpful."

Topics in This Chapter

- Finding Your Place Again
- Seeing Changes in Those Important to You
- Encountering Anxiety in Others
- ↻ Finding Things to Talk About
- Influence of Culture on Developing Friendships
- ↻ Cultivating Friendships
- Returning to What Was Once Normal
- ↻ Glean and Go Forward

Take a moment to ask Him for wisdom as you continue your *Returning Well* journey.

Finding Your Place Again

From your perspective in re-entry, in what ways have those with whom you were close before you left your primary culture released their connection to you?

In what ways have the roles that you used to fill in your primary culture been filled by others?[1]

What have these experiences from the previous two questions been like for you?

If desired and appropriate, what are some healthy ways that you could re-engage these relationships?

What other roles are now available for you to fill because of your season of life that you lived cross-culturally?

Take a moment to ask Him which of these roles He would desire you to fill in this coming season, and then circle them.

---

[1] On the plane, Stan tells Chuck about the funeral they had for him. At Kelly's house, Chuck sees how his role in her life has been filled by someone else.

Seeing Changes in Those Important to You

Consider those you were close to prior to moving to your primary culture. How have their lives most dramatically changed during the time that you lived cross-culturally? From which of their significant life events, if any, were you absent?[2]

What effects have these changes and missed events had on you as well as on your relationships with these close family members and friends?

You

Your relationships

What adjustments, if any, would be helpful for you to make based on these changes and missed events? What might be some helpful next steps you could take to make these adjustments?

Encountering Anxiety in Others

How might others feel anxious around you now that you have returned?[3]

→

---

[2] Chuck realizes that Stan's wife died and that Kelly is a mother.
[3] Kelly makes Chuck coffee, and as he tersely starts a sentence, she tenses.

For meeting

Given these anxieties, how might you help others feel comfortable around you?

Finding things to talk about is like identifying stepping stones to the other side of the river: Those taking the effort to do so will soon learn the joy of discovering an unexplored world and potentially even the opportunity for sharing their own.

Finding Things to Talk About

Consider the topics that you perceive are important to people in your primary culture.[4] What might be some areas of common interest that you share with them?

Create five open-ended questions (i.e., questions that cannot be answered with a yes or no response) that you would be comfortable using as conversation starters with others in your primary culture.

1.

2.

3.

4.

5.

---

[4] Chuck asks Kelly about a football team and then about her doctorate.

Influence of Culture on Developing Friendships

How has the process of developing friendships in your primary culture differed from the process of developing friendships in your host culture?

What has been most challenging about initiating and developing friendships in your primary culture since your return? What are some ways that you could positively address this challenge?

Cultivating Friendships

What types of friendships will be the most important for you to intentionally cultivate over this coming year (such as a walking/running/exercise buddy, close confidant, professional peer, fellow parent, or friendships with those in a small group or service group, etc.)?

How much time and effort would you expect it to take to cultivate each of these friendships?

→

CORE TOPIC

Friendships in re-entry are like streams of water in a desert, refreshing the soul and giving strength to carry on: Finding them is worth the effort.

How might you go about finding and cultivating these friendships?

Returning to What Was Once Normal

What normal primary-culture experiences—which you did not have while in your host culture—are you now experiencing again?[5]

What has most surprised you, if anything, about these experiences?

CORE TOPIC

Questions & Insights

Glean and Go Forward

Once you have completed this chapter to your satisfaction, take a moment to review your responses, taking note of the following:

- Identify one valuable item, i.e., something that stands out to you, holds meaning for you, has a strong emotional impact on you, or you sense Him bringing to your attention. Record it on p. 171.

- Next, identify anything you sense Him leading you to know or do based on this chapter. Record it on p. 173.

- Finally, identify which questions you would like to explore and insights you would like to share with your companion. Star them or jot them to the left.

[5] Chuck gets into his vehicle and drives again.

CHAPTER SIXTEEN

Debriefing Closure

How did *Returning Well* make a difference in your re-entry?

"Returning Well kept me focused on processing re-entry. It did not allow me to just slip into busy American life without thinking through where I've been and where He is calling me to be next."

What were some of your most poignant take-aways from engaging *Returning Well*?

"That what I learned there is still applicable and necessary here, that we won't be the same and, in fact, are always changing throughout life (even if we were to stay in the same place), so we don't have to be surprised or disappointed if things are changing, that some things we dreamed might never happen, and that the more involved I am here the less I will miss being there."

Topics in This Chapter

- Your *Returning Well* Companion
- Accepting Paradoxes
- Reaching Healthy Closure
- Enjoying Your Unique Cultural Blend
- Re-Entry Thankfulness
- Possibilities, Hopes, and Objectives
- Glean and Go Forward

Take a moment to ask Him for wisdom as you continue your *Returning Well* journey.

Your *Returning Well* Companion

Consider the meetings that you have had with your *Returning Well* Companion. What has been most helpful from your time with him or her thus far?[1]

How might you express your appreciation to your companion for his or her help?

Accepting paradoxes is like being willing to see the glass half full and half empty—both at the same time— and thus see things as they really are, or really were.

Accepting Paradoxes

What paradoxes did you encounter during the time you lived cross-culturally?

As you reflect on these paradoxes now, what stands out to you?

What paradoxes are you currently encountering in your re-entry transition?[2]

---

[1] Stan helps Chuck process his experiences.
[2] Chuck accepts his emotional paradox regarding Kelly: He is sad about losing her but is glad she was with him on the island.

What would it look like for you to accept these re-entry paradoxes?

What difference would accepting them make?

What do you mean by "paradoxes"? ▶ Paradoxes are emotions or experiences that are seemingly contradictory yet exist together. For instance, a wedding can cause both celebratory toasts and silent prayers for endurance, a new baby might bring both unspeakable joy and trepidation, and the death of an aging relative may initiate both the pain of grief and a sigh of relief. Likewise, paradoxes are a common experience for cross-cultural sojourners.

Reaching Healthy Closure

Imagine that you have reached a sense of healthy closure on your recent season of cross-cultural service.[3] How would others know that you have reached this closure —what would they notice about you?

What difference would reaching this healthy closure make in your next season of life?

→

---

[3] As Chuck talks with Stan, he reaches a sense of closure.

If you have not yet reached this place of healthy closure, what else would help you reach it?

CORE TOPIC

Enjoying your unique cultural blend is like celebrating where the yellows of your host culture meet the blues of your primary culture and mix together into lovely greens in your very person, creating beauty, uniqueness, nuance, and vitality.

Enjoying Your Unique Cultural Blend

What are the most obvious ways the cultures you have lived in are blending together into who you are now?[4]

How have the various cultural attributes you have internalized drawn you to certain people and activities in your primary culture during this season of re-entry?

What might help you thrive with your unique cultural blend in the coming season?

---

[4] Delivering the package, Chuck exhibits a new personal culture that blends his host and primary cultures. His new blend is faster than the island but more relaxed than before it, and now he has two friends with him: Wilson and Elvis.

Assuming that He purposefully gave you this unique cultural blend, what value do you think it might have for His Kingdom in this next season?

Re-Entry Thankfulness

CORE TOPIC

As you consider your season of re-entry, for what are you thankful?

Expressing thankfulness can be like an acquired taste: At first it may feel foreign and forced, then it becomes awkward yet intriguing, and finally it becomes habitual and relished.

How might you meaningfully express your thankfulness?

Possibilities, Hopes, and Objectives

CORE TOPIC

How has your time spent cross-culturally produced and/or illuminated new possibilities in your primary culture that you may not have noticed otherwise?[5]

Like a recharge to a nearly-empty cellphone battery are the hopes, dreams, and vision for the next season of life, providing in part the energy to make connections and move forward into the future.

→

[5] At a crossroads, Chuck looks at his map, gets directions, and considers which way to go next.

For meeting

  4

What hopes and longings do you have for this coming season?

Take a moment to bring these hopes and longings before your loving and gracious Creator.

What objectives have you considered pursuing in this upcoming season?

What values are most important to you as you consider these possibilities, hopes, longings, and objectives?

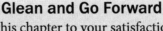

CORE TOPIC

Questions & Insights

Glean and Go Forward

Once you have completed this chapter to your satisfaction, take a moment to review your responses, taking note of the following:

- Identify one valuable item, i.e., something that stands out to you, holds meaning for you, has a strong emotional impact on you, or you sense Him bringing to your attention. Record it on p. 171.

- Next, identify anything you sense Him leading you to know or do based on this chapter. Record it on p. 173.

- Finally, identify which questions you would like to explore and insights you would like to share with your companion. Star them or jot them to the left.

CHAPTER SEVENTEEN

Specific Experience: Single Life

What about *Returning Well* was most powerful and effective for you?

"Being able to think about specifics instead of just, 'Life here is crazy and has turned on its head.'"

What was most enjoyable about engaging *Returning Well* for you?

"Having a resource to go to when I needed a perspective check."

Topics in This Chapter

- Host-Culture Living as a Single
- Host-Culture Gender Expectations
- Colleague Expectations
- Team Dynamics
- Marriage
- Thankfulness
- Glean and Go Forward

Take a moment to ask Him for wisdom as you continue your *Returning Well* journey.

CORE TOPIC

Serving as a single person is a lot like taking the back roads while many others take the interstate: We have the same destination, but it is the road far less traveled—having unique difficulties (like being stopped by trains or sent on long detours), but also amazing discoveries (like quaint cafés or fascinating bridges) that would have otherwise been missed.[1]

Host-Culture Living as a Single

What were some of the greatest advantages of being single in your host culture? What did you enjoy most about these advantages?

What difficulties did you face in your host culture specifically because of your singleness? How did these difficulties affect the way you viewed being single?

What advice would you give to a transitioning cross-cultural sojourner regarding how to thrive as a single person living cross-culturally?

Circle any aspects of this advice that might be helpful to you as you seek to thrive in your primary culture.

Host-Culture Gender Expectations

What expectations did your host culture have of singles of your age and gender?

---

[1] Adapted from R.H., who has been serving cross-culturally as a single for eight years.

How did you respond to these expectations, both inwardly and outwardly?

Inwardly

Outwardly

How did these expectations affect your interactions with others as well as your view of yourself?

Interactions with others

View of yourself

Colleague Expectations

What expectations did your colleagues have of you because of your singleness?

How did you handle these expectations?

$\rightarrow$

What expectations might others have of you in this coming season of life because of your singleness?

What will help you to handle these expectations well?

Team Dynamics

What was your role on your team (or in your work-group), both in title and in practice?

How did you handle any discrepancies between what you thought your role was supposed to be and your actual responsibilities?

If you were to describe the dynamics of your team in three words, what words would you choose? What about your team makes these three words appropriate?

How did your team most encourage you?

What contributed to your team functioning well? What, if anything, regularly thwarted the functioning of your team?

Contributed to your team functioning well	*Thwarted the functioning of your team*

What wisdom do you want to take forward from these team experiences into the next season and any future team(s)?

For meeting

Marriage

How has your cross-cultural experience as a single person influenced your view of marriage?

When, if ever, did you consider pursuing a relationship with the thought of marriage while working cross-culturally? What influenced your decision regarding whether or not to pursue such a relationship?

What future hopes do you have as you consider singleness and marriage?

CORE TOPIC

Giving thanks is a gift —sometimes prompted by feeling, sometimes prompted by will—but a gift, nonetheless, that gives you back more than you originally gave.

Thankfulness

When you consider the unique influence that cross-cultural living as a single has had on you, for what do you want to give thanks?

Glean and Go Forward

Once you have completed this chapter to your satisfaction, take a moment to review your responses, taking note of the following:

- Identify one valuable item, i.e., something that stands out to you, holds meaning for you, has a strong emotional impact on you, or you sense Him bringing to your attention. Record it on p. 171.

- Next, identify anything you sense Him leading you to know or do based on this chapter. Record it on p. 173.

- Finally, identify which questions you would like to explore and insights you would like to share with your companion. Star them or jot them to the right.

CORE TOPIC

Questions & Insights

For meeting

CHAPTER EIGHTEEN

Specific Experience: Married Life

"The 'Married Life' chapter was great. Practical, deep, and positive."

"In the married chapter, I appreciated the questions that focused on thinking through how to affirm my spouse in these various areas..."

What were some of your most poignant take-aways from engaging *Returning Well*?

"Greater appreciation for my husband."

Topics in This Chapter

A Focus on Transition
- **Desire and Decision to Leave**
- **Transition and Your Spouse**

A Focus on Cross-Cultural Living
- **Team Dynamics**
- **Expectations of Culture**
- **Enjoying Time Together**
- **Valuing Your Spouse**
- **Conflicts in Your Marriage**
- **Sexual Intimacy**
- **Collaboration with Your Spouse**

- **Admiring Your Spouse**
- **Expressing Faith Together**
- **Marriage Growth**

A Focus on Re-Entry
- **Handling Re-Entry Stressors**
- **Supporting Your Spouse through Grief**
- **Re-Entry Shock-Absorbers**

- **Glean and Go Forward**

Take a moment to ask Him for wisdom as you continue your *Returning Well* journey.

get the most

In addition to utilizing the guidance from the "Get the Most out of Part Two: 'Inquiring'" page, further optimize your *Returning Well* journey through this chapter by **first individually engaging** applicable topics and questions before **jointly engaging** with your spouse the questions you believe would be beneficial to discuss together.

Also, note that the questions assume that you and your spouse jointly moved to a host culture different from your primary culture. If this does not describe your circumstance, please consider the host culture in this chapter to be the culture from which you have recently departed and the primary culture to be the culture to which you have recently moved. Finally, note that if you have a cross-cultural marriage, you may need to alter some of the questions to fit your situation.

A Focus on Transition

Desire and Decision to Leave

When you were initially considering moving to your host culture, how would you have described your desire to move to your host culture in comparison to your spouse's?

How were you able to work through any differences in desire to move that you and your spouse had?

How did the two of you decide to move to your host culture? What impact did this decision-making process have on how each of you adjusted to your host culture?

Transition and Your Spouse

What concerns did your spouse most frequently voice during transition?

From your perspective, how did the stress of cross-cultural adjustment affect your spouse?

How has this awareness from the previous two questions influenced how you care for and relate to your spouse?

A Focus on Cross-Cultural Living

Team Dynamics

What were your and your spouse's roles on your team(s) (or in your work-group(s)), both in title and in practice? How did you handle any discrepancies between what you thought your roles were supposed to be and your actual responsibilities?

$\rightarrow$

For meeting

What were some of the most significant expectations that these teams had of you and your spouse? In what ways did your responses to these expectations regularly affect your marriage?

How did your team encourage your marriage?

What contributed to your team functioning well? What, if anything, regularly thwarted the functioning of your team?

Contributed to your team functioning well	Thwarted the functioning of your team

What wisdom do you want to take forward from these team experiences into the next season and any future team(s)?

Expectations of Culture

What expectations did your host culture have for how spouses should relate to one another? How did you personally respond to these expectations?

How did these expectations influence your interactions with your spouse in public and in private?

In public

In private

What expectations does your primary culture now have for how you should relate to your spouse?

In what ways have these primary-culture expectations been rejuvenating to you, if at all? In what ways have these expectations been loathsome, if at all?

Rejuvenating	*Loathsome*

→

What would help you and your spouse to navigate well the changes in expectations that your marriage is experiencing?

Enjoying Time Together

How did your host culture influence the quantity and quality of time you enjoyed with your spouse?

How did you enjoy spending time with your spouse in your host culture? How would you enjoy spending time with your spouse in this next season of life?

In host culture

In next season of life

CORE TOPIC

Showing your spouse his or her importance to you in a way that makes the most sense to him or her is like providing an oasis in the desert,

(continued next page)

Valuing Your Spouse

What were you doing when your spouse most felt loved, respected, and valued by you during this recent season?

What things, if any, regularly hindered your efforts to show your spouse his or her importance to you?

(continued from previous) *a refuge in the storm, and a fresh breeze in a musty basement: It may not eradicate the adversities, but it sure does make them more bearable.*

Circle any of these that might be challenges to showing your spouse his or her importance to you in this coming season.

How could you show your spouse his or her importance to you in a way that is meaningful to him or her in this next season of life?

Conflicts in Your Marriage

What conflicts did you most frequently encounter in your marriage while living cross-culturally? How were you able to work through these conflicts?

What do you like about the way that you currently handle conflicts? How would you like the way you handle conflicts with your spouse to improve?

What you like	*Ways to improve*

For meeting

Sexual Intimacy

How did cross-cultural living influence your sexual intimacy?

What did you learn about each other sexually while living cross-culturally?

On a scale of one to ten (with ten being "connecting and pleasurable," and one being "distancing and disappointing"), where would you rate your sexual intimacy? Where do you think your spouse would rate your sexual intimacy?

You   *Your spouse*

What is one action that you could take that has the potential to maintain and/or enhance your sexual intimacy during this season of re-entry?

Collaboration with Your Spouse

What is one particular instance where you experienced great collaboration with your spouse while serving cross-culturally?

What about that situation allowed you and your spouse to work together so well?

What can you glean from this experience that might help you and your spouse work together well in this coming season?

Admiring Your Spouse

From your perspective, in what ways did your spouse flourish in your host culture?

What do you admire about your spouse as you consider this recent season of cross-cultural service?

How could you communicate to your spouse your admiration in a way that is meaningful to him or her?

CORE TOPIC

Expressing faith together in the next season is like opening a book to a new chapter: The story continues, and there is a fresh opportunity for the characters to stay connected and strive toward a common purpose.

Expressing Faith Together

What do you appreciate about how your spouse's faith was expressed while living cross-culturally?

What were some of the most meaningful ways that your spouse encouraged your faith while living cross-culturally?

What hopes do you have for how your faith will jointly be expressed in the coming season of life after re-entry?

CORE TOPIC

Just as a plant turns its leaves to face the sunshine each time it is moved to a different location, so a thriving marriage makes adjustments to continue growing with each transition it makes.

Marriage Growth

In what ways did your marriage grow the most while in your host culture?

What advice would you give to a transitioning married couple as to how to thrive cross-culturally?

Circle any aspects of this advice that might be helpful to you as you seek to thrive in your primary culture.

As you consider ways in which you would like your marriage to grow in this coming season, what do you sense Him leading you to make a priority? How might you go about doing so?

A Focus on Re-Entry

Handling Re-Entry Stressors

CORE TOPIC

What stressors have been most challenging for your spouse during re-entry? How has your spouse responded to these stressors?

For every action, there is a reaction, and together they create an interaction. It only takes one change of action to get a new reaction and change your entire interaction.[1]

---

[1] Adapted from Miller, Sherod and Phyllis Miller. *Couple Communication Instructor Manual.* Evergreen, CO: Interpersonal Communication Programs, 2007.

For meeting

  4

What effect does your spouse's response to his or her stressors have on you?

Consider the seven significant stressors you listed on p. 79. How have you responded to your stressors?

How does your response to your stressors affect your spouse?

How could the two of you jointly handle the stress of re-entry more effectively?

Supporting Your Spouse through Grief

What losses from this recent transition have been most difficult for your spouse? From your perspective, how has your spouse begun to grieve these losses?

What can you do to practically yet compassionately help your spouse grieve well?

Re-Entry Shock-Absorbers

How have your and your spouse's daily responsibilities most significantly changed upon re-entry?

What is one practical thing that each of you could do to support each other through these adjustments?

One practical thing I could do to support my spouse

One practical thing my spouse could do to support me

As you consider this recent transition, what do you most appreciate about your spouse? For what are you most thankful?

→

CORE TOPIC

Going through re-entry without support, gratitude, appreciation, and celebration is like driving on a bumpy road without shock-absorbers: It leaves you feeling sore, exhausted, and ready for a distinct change.

How might you communicate your appreciation and gratitude to your spouse in a way that is encouraging to him or her?

As you consider the re-entry experiences you have had as a couple, what do you want to celebrate? How might you go about doing so?

Glean and Go Forward

Once you have completed this chapter to your satisfaction, take a moment to review your responses, taking note of the following:

- Identify one valuable item, i.e., something that stands out to you, holds meaning for you, has a strong emotional impact on you, or you sense Him bringing to your attention. Record it on p. 171.

- Next, identify anything you sense Him leading you to know or do based on this chapter. Record it on p. 173.

- Now, identify which questions you would like to use as conversation starters with your spouse. Mark them with a diamond or jot them below.

- Finally, considering what is best for your marriage, identify which questions you would like to explore and insights you would like to share with your companion. Star them or jot them to the left.

CHAPTER NINETEEN

Specific Experience: Parenting

"This chapter really helped me to focus on my children and what they were feeling with adjustment also. The questions about expectations of each culture really helped me to pinpoint where adjustment would need to be made so that I could be gracious to my daughter as she navigated those waters."

"I enjoyed this chapter as it helped me process my family's returning through my children's eyes and mindset."

Topics in This Chapter

A Focus on Transition
- **Your Child's Special Belongings**
- ⟳ **Transition Stress and Your Child**

A Focus on Cross-Cultural Life
- ⟳ **Host-Culture Influence on Parenting**
- **Pressure to Behave**
- **Struggles and Joys of Cross-Cultural Living**
- **Conflicts with Your Child**
- **Your Child's Education**
- **Your Child's View of Education**
- **Sibling(s)**
- ⟳ **Admiring Your Child**
- ⟳ **Valuing Your Child**

A Focus on Departure and Re-Entry
- **Your Child's Goodbyes**
- ⟳ **Grieving Transition Losses**
- ⟳ **Adjusting to Parent's Primary Culture**
- ⟳ **Navigating Cultural Expectations**
- **Family Activities and Traditions**
- ⟳ **Thanks and Celebration**

A Focus for You and Your Child
- ⟳ **Questions to Consider with Your Child**

- ⟳ **Glean and Go Forward**

Take a moment to ask Him for wisdom as you continue your *Returning Well* journey.

get the most

In addition to utilizing the guidance from the "Get the Most out of Part Two: 'Inquiring'" page, further optimize your *Returning Well* journey through this chapter by **first individually engaging** applicable topics and questions, and then by setting aside time(s) to **jointly engage** with your child(ren) the topic, "Questions to Consider *with* Your Child," as well as any other topics that would be of interest to both of you. Further, to best understand the questions in this chapter, note the following:

- The questions refer to "child" instead of "children." If you have multiple children, consider the question you are engaging for each child.
- A child's internal/felt primary culture may be a conglomeration of cultures and often depends on several factors including, but not limited to, the following: the timing of their transition(s), their appearance, the cultures in which they have lived as well as the duration in each, and their parents' primary culture(s). Thus, when the following questions refer to "primary culture" and "host culture," they are referring to your—the parent's—primary and host cultures.
- For ease in readability, this chapter uses the plural "they" and "their" to refer to singular antecedents.

A Focus on Transition

Your Child's Special Belongings

What belongings have been most difficult for your child to leave behind as they have transitioned cultures?

What special belongings has your child taken with them during each transition? What significance does each of these items have to your child?

Transition Stress and Your Child

What concerns did your child most frequently voice during transition?

From your perspective, how did the stress of transition affect your child?

How does this awareness from the previous two questions influence how you parent your child?

A Focus on Cross-Cultural Life

Host-Culture Influence on Parenting

What did your host culture seem to value the most when it came to parenting?

In what ways did your host culture influence the way you parented?

→

For meeting

Which parenting habits or values that you developed while living in your host culture would you like to continue utilizing going forward, if any?

Pressure to Behave

In what ways did you feel pressure to make your child behave in a certain way while living cross-culturally? What was different about the times you handled these pressures well?

How did these pressures and your responses to them affect your relationship with your child?

In what ways are you feeling pressure to make your child behave in a certain way in re-entry? If your friend were in the exact same situation as you, how would you advise them to respond, both to their child as well as to those providing the pressure?

Struggles and Joys of Cross-Cultural Living

What struggles and joys did your child face in the following areas because of cross-cultural living? Use the following page to consider specific areas of joy and struggle.

Struggles	Joys
Social/Relational	
Spiritual/Faith walk	
Personal identity	
Educational	
Linguistic	
Physical	

→

For meeting

How did your child's cross-cultural struggles and joys personally affect you? How did they affect your relationship with your child?

You

Your relationship

Conflicts with Your Child

What conflicts did you most frequently encounter in your relationship with your child while living cross-culturally? How were you able to work through these conflicts?

How would you like the way you handle conflicts with your child to improve during this next season of life?

Your Child's Education

What were your highest values as you considered your child's educational options while you served in your host culture? Given these values, how pleased are you with the education your child has received thus far?

What are some of your highest values as you consider your child's educational options in this coming season of life?

Your Child's View of Education

What would your child say about their education? What might your child request to be different about their education going forward?

What educational hopes and dreams does your child have? Which of these might you accommodate?

Sibling(s)

In what ways did cross-cultural living shape your child's relationship(s) with their sibling(s)?

How has this recent transition affected your child's sibling relationship(s)?

→

For meeting

In what ways do you desire your child's relationship(s) with their sibling(s) to grow in this next season of life? What steps could you take to encourage this desired growth?

CORE TOPIC

Like a gust of wind that swells the sail of a sailboat is an apt affirmation to the heart of a child, filling their heart with love, hope, confidence, and courage that further propels them forward into their future.

Admiring Your Child

Which of your child's cross-cultural feats brings them the most satisfaction?

What do you admire about your child as you consider this recent season of cross-cultural living?

How can you express your admiration to your child in a way that is meaningful to them?

CORE TOPIC

Like an airport terminal to an airplane is a parent valuing their child: In sunny weather it provides a launching place from which to

(continued next page)

Valuing Your Child

What were you doing when your child most felt loved, nurtured, and valued by you during this recent season?

What things, if any, regularly hindered your efforts to show your child their importance to you?

(continued from previous) *venture out, and in stormy weather it is a safe place to find refuge, re-fueling, and rest.*

Circle any of these that might be challenges to showing your child their importance to you in this coming season.

How could you show your child their importance to you in a way that is meaningful to them in this next season of life?

A Focus on Departure and Re-Entry

Your Child's Goodbyes

Which people, places, things (including animals), and aspects of culture were most important to your child in your host culture? What made each important? If your child said goodbye, how did they say goodbye to each? How did this goodbye most predominately affect them?

Most important ____ and what made each important to your child	How your child said goodbye and how this goodbye most predominately affected them
People	

→

Most important ___ and what made each important to your child	How your child said goodbye and how this goodbye most predominately affected them
Places	
Things	
Aspects of culture	

To which important people, places, things, or aspects of culture did your child not have an opportunity to say goodbye? How can you help your child say goodbye to them now?

What, if anything, would improve the goodbye process for your child the next time they transition?

Grieving Transition Losses

What losses from this recent transition have been most difficult for your child? From your perspective, how has your child begun to grieve these losses?

What can you do to practically and compassionately help your child grieve well?

Ignoring a child's grief is like ignoring a child's skinned knee: Attentive care hastens healing whereas minimizing the injury risks infection and a long-term scar.

Adjusting to Parent's Primary Culture

What aspects of your primary culture have been perplexing to your child upon re-entry?

How has your child responded to any cultural mistakes they have made?

What life skills does your child need to learn or further develop in order to thrive in this next season of life?

Adjusting to my parent's primary culture sometimes feels like I am expected to pass an exam for a class I never took.

→

Given your responses to the previous questions in this topic, who might serve as a helpful cultural mentor for your child during re-entry?

Navigating Cultural Expectations

What were the most significant expectations those in your host culture had of your child? What are the most significant expectations those in your primary culture currently have of your child?

Expectations in host culture	*Expectations in primary culture*

How can you help your child navigate the changes in expectations they are experiencing?

Family Activities and Traditions

Which regular family activities or traditions did your child most enjoy in your host culture?

Circle which of these activities or traditions are most important to your child to continue doing.

What would it take for you to practically incorporate these circled items into your family life in the coming season?

Thanks and Celebration

As you consider how this re-entry has affected your child, for what are you most thankful?

When you consider your child's re-entry, what do you most want to celebrate? How might you go about celebrating these things with your child in a way that they would also enjoy?

CORE TOPIC

Sharing thanks and celebrations is like sharing dessert: Everyone ends up with a sweet taste in their mouth.

For meeting

 3 **4** 5 6

A Focus for You and Your Child

One of Love's most potent embodiments is patient and genuine listening.

Questions to Consider *with* Your Child

Adapt the following questions to your child's age and stage, and then use them as conversation starters with your child in environments that are most comfortable for them.

Home
- When do you feel like you are home? What makes you feel that way?
- Where do you want to live when you get older? What would make that place feel like home?

Cross-cultural living
- What do you like about each place you have lived?
- What is something that someone thought you should know, but you didn't know? What was that like for you?

Change
- In what ways do you enjoy change? In what ways do you not like change?
- What things about you stay the same as you change cultures and locations?

This transition
- What have you liked about this transition? What has surprised you?
- What about this transition has made you sad? What has made you angry?

Friendship/Belonging
- What do you look for in a friend?
- Who are your closest friends? What do you like about each person?

Family
- When do you most enjoy our family? What do you enjoy about it?
- If you could change one thing about our family, what would you change? What do you like about that change?

Hopes
- What are you looking forward to in this coming year? What do you hope will happen?
- How would you like me to be a part of that, if at all?

Our relationship
- How well do you feel that I understand you and what you are experiencing?
- What is something that you wish I understood about you?

Glean and Go Forward

Once you have completed this chapter to your satisfaction, take a moment to review your responses, taking note of the following:

- Identify one valuable item, i.e., something that stands out to you, holds meaning for you, has a strong emotional impact on you, or you sense Him bringing to your attention. Record it on p. 171.

- Next, identify anything you sense Him leading you to know or do based on this chapter. Record it on p. 173.

- Now, identify any additional questions you would like to use as conversation starters with your child. Mark them with a diamond or jot them below.

- Finally, keeping in mind what would be respectful of your child and best for your relationship with them, identify which questions you would like to explore and insights you would like to share with your companion. Star them or jot them to the right.

CORE TOPIC

Questions & Insights

For meeting

PART THREE

Integrating

A glimpse of what is ahead...

"[I am] defining new goals and being intentional about reaching them."

"I am able to build upon things for the future from what I have learned from my past experiences."

"I expect to be, and already am, more intentional, more focused on having purpose and direction in this new season, more articulate in sharing lessons from the years overseas, and more equipped to help others as they go through similar transitions."

Get the Most out of Part Three: "Integrating"

Optimize your *Returning Well* journey through Part Three: "Integrating" by engaging the topics in the following ways:

Engage according to your method (such as journaling, reflecting, drawing, talking with others, etc.).

Engage with clarity on the season of service you are addressing.

Engage at your chosen pace using your chosen approach.

If you are using the	and <u>any</u> of the approaches,
six-week pace,	consider on average two core topics each day, and then Chapter Twenty-Two during the following week.
three-month pace,	consider on average one core topic each day and then Chapter Twenty-Two during the following two weeks.
six-month pace,	consider on average three core topics each week and then Chapter Twenty-Two during the following month.

Engage by maintaining a conversational yet humble posture. Ask Him for wisdom and sensitivity to His leading with every topic and question.

Engage with freedom to skip any topics or questions that you do not sense Him leading you to respond to, that do not apply to you, or that do not interest you.

Further enhance your engagement of Part Three: "Integrating" by meeting with your companion. Following is the suggested plan for your meetings:

- During Meeting **5**, share from Chapter Twenty through Chapter Twenty-One.

- During Meeting **6**, share from Chapter Twenty-Two and bring closure to your time together by celebrating key insights gained and solidifying next steps.

get the most

You are almost there! You have done the hard work of gleaning treasures, and now you're ready to hone them, refine them, and discern how to put them to good use to fully reach a DYNAMIC renewal!

CHAPTER TWENTY

Gathering to Gain Insight

What helped you to get the most out of your *Returning Well* engagement?

"[It was] helpful for me to have the list from Chapter Twenty that I developed as I went along to look over at the end for applying significant insights. Because I went through the material over such a long period of time, I would have forgotten a lot of my thoughts and not been able to pull out themes and patterns if I hadn't used that format."

Topics In This Chapter

⟳ **Gathering Valuable Items**   ⟳ **Evaluating Debriefing**

Take a moment
to ask Him for wisdom
as you continue your
Returning Well journey.

CORE TOPIC

Gathering your valuable items is like collecting random notes of music and preparing them to be crafted into a magnificent musical score that will give expression to your song of this recent season.

Gathering Valuable Items

Throughout Part Two: "Inquiring," each chapter contains a core topic titled, "Glean and Go Forward." Those core topics contain instructions to record one valuable item (i.e., something that stands out to you, holds meaning for you, has a strong emotional impact on you, or you sense Him bringing to your attention) and anything you sense Him leading you to know or do based on that chapter. As you survey pp. 170–173 and find blank spaces for Chapter Three through Chapter Sixteen and any applicable chapters after that, consider reviewing your responses from those particular chapters and discerning any missing valuable items and also things you're feeling led to know or do. Once you're satisfied with your responses on these pages, then continue to the next core topic in this chapter.

Chapter	Valuable Items
Chapter Three **Departure and Initial Transition** pp. 19–25	
Chapter Four **A Dream Come True?** pp. 27–34	
Chapter Five **Accepting and Adapting** pp. 35–42	
Chapter Six **Relationships and Communication** pp. 43–50	
Chapter Seven **Cross-Cultural Living** pp. 51–56	
Chapter Eight **Sojourner Truths** pp. 57–66	
Chapter Nine **Proficiency and Completion** pp. 67–73	

Valuable Items	Chapter
	Chapter Ten **Appreciating Adversity** *pp. 75–83*
	Chapter Eleven **Leaving** *pp. 85–91*
	Chapter Twelve **Back "Home"?** *pp. 93–98*
	Chapter Thirteen **Re-Integrating** *pp. 99–106*
	Chapter Fourteen **Recognizing Change** *pp. 107–113*
	Chapter Fifteen **Re-Connecting** *pp. 115–120*
	Chapter Sixteen **Debriefing Closure** *pp. 121–126*
	Chapter Seventeen **Single Life** *pp. 127–133*
	Chapter Eighteen **Married Life** *pp. 135–148*
	Chapter Nineteen **Parenting** *pp. 149–163*

For meeting

    2 3 4 **5** 6

Chapter	What you sense Him leading you to know or do
Chapter Three **Departure and Initial Transition** pp. 19–25	
Chapter Four **A Dream Come True?** pp. 27–34	
Chapter Five **Accepting and Adapting** pp. 35–42	
Chapter Six **Relationships and Communication** pp. 43–50	
Chapter Seven **Cross-Cultural Living** pp. 51–56	
Chapter Eight **Sojourner Truths** pp. 57–66	
Chapter Nine **Proficiency and Completion** pp. 67–73	
Chapter Ten **Appreciating Adversity** pp. 75–83	
Chapter Eleven **Leaving** pp. 85–91	

What you sense Him leading you to know or do	Chapter
	Chapter Twelve **Back "Home"?** *pp. 93–98*
	Chapter Thirteen **Re-Integrating** *pp. 99–106*
	Chapter Fourteen **Recognizing Change** *pp. 107–113*
	Chapter Fifteen **Re-Connecting** *pp. 115–120*
	Chapter Sixteen **Debriefing Closure** *pp. 121–126*
	Chapter Seventeen **Single Life** *pp. 127–133*
	Chapter Eighteen **Married Life** *pp. 135–148*
	Chapter Nineteen **Parenting** *pp. 149–163*

For meeting

2 3 4 **5** 6

CORE TOPIC

Quitting the process of debriefing to reach renewal before it is complete is like taking weeks to plan the vacation of a lifetime—securing guides, purchasing tour and travel tickets, finding just the right place to stay, procuring appropriate clothing—and then once you land at your destination, you decide staying at the airport is good enough.

Evaluating Debriefing

An **effective debriefing** is reflecting on a recent season of life in order to process the specific aspects of it (events, experiences, emotions, decisions, relationships, thoughts, and actions), understand its impact personally and communally, recognize and accept its paradoxes, identify personal growth and things learned, and bring about a meaningful closure. Effective debriefing naturally leads to renewal.

Given the definition above, on a scale of one to ten, how close would you say that you are to completing the debriefing process (with ten being, "I am satisfied with my progress and am ready to move forward," and one being, "I still have work to do.")?

If your response was not at least an eight, what remains for you in the debriefing process?

CHAPTER TWENTY-ONE

Applying Significant Insights

Which questions were most memorable and/or helpful?

"Chapter Twenty-One as a whole was really good; it tied it together. I liked the process of finding themes, determining insights, imagining application, and final encapsulation."

"Application questions. These were meaningful because there is a sense of capturing those things that I love about living cross-culturally and moving them with me."

What about Returning Well was most powerful and effective for you?

"Thinking through what we actually accomplished while serving cross-culturally and creating specific goals now that we are back to stay."

Topics in This Chapter

A Focus on Honing Insights
- ○ Themes and Patterns in Gleanings
- ○ Determining Your Five Most Significant Insights
- ○ Imagining Application

A Focus on Applying Insights Practically
- ○ Clarifying Your Goal

- ○ Valuing Your Goal
- ○ Determining Action Steps
- ○ Preparing to Succeed

A Focus on Culmination
- ○ Final Encapsulation
- ○ Reaching a Dynamic Renewal

- ○ Glean and Go Forward

Take a moment to ask Him for wisdom as you continue your *Returning Well* journey.

A Focus on Honing Insights

Although the starry night sky is beautiful regardless, discovering themes and patterns is like learning astronomy: Those same stars now appear as purposeful parts of a larger whole, and they also become useful for future navigation.

recognize

Themes and Patterns in Gleanings

As you look back over the items you collected on pp. 170–173 in Chapter Twenty, what themes and patterns do you see?

What do these themes and patterns reveal about how He has made you (such as your calling, gifts, skills, strengths, hopes, challenges, personality, and temperament)?

What do these themes and patterns reveal about His work in and through your life during this recent season of living cross-culturally?

What do these themes and patterns reveal about the meaning of this recent season of life that you lived in your host culture?

How might recognizing these themes and patterns influence the following areas of your life in your next season?

How you love, serve, and adore your Creator

Your relationships with others

The decisions you make

Determining Your Five Most Significant Insights

As you consider all of your gleanings from Chapter Twenty as well as your responses to the previous topic, "Themes and Patterns in Gleanings," what five insights do you perceive are most significant?

1.

2.

3.

4.

5.

→

CORE TOPIC

Determining your most significant insights is like packing your carry-on: You are deciding what is most important to have with you at all times as you embark on your next journey.

crystalize

What is the significance of each of these insights, for you, for others, and/or for the Kingdom?

1.

2.

3.

4.

5.

CORE TOPIC

Imagining application of your insights and having a sense of what it would take to integrate them is like hiking a trail while at the same time seeing clearly the peak to which the trail leads: You have both the vision of where you are going and the direction to get you there.

Imagining Application

Imagine yourself in this coming season of life after re-entry. You've reached a sense of normality in your primary culture. What might a typical day look like for you? What challenges do you expect to regularly face? What do you think you'll look forward to in any given week? What activities do you think He will want you to give your attention to on a regular basis?

Now imagine, in the same scenario as the previous question, that you are integrating your five significant insights into your life in such a way that they are benefiting yourself and others as well as bringing honor to your Creator. In what specific ways is each insight making a difference day-to-day?

1.

2.

3.

4.

5.

Continue to imagine yourself in the next season of life. Your fully integrated insights are making the positive differences you described in the previous question. Now imagine that a friend asks you what it took for you to reach this place. As you look back and consider all that has transpired, what would you say? What did it take for you to reach this place?

For meeting

  4 5 6

A Focus on Applying Insights Practically

Clarifying Your Goal

As you reflect on your responses in this chapter thus far, what aspirations or goals do you sense Him leading you to work toward?

Of the aspirations or goals you wrote above, ask Him which one He would desire that you work toward first and circle it.

Clarify your goal as much as possible. State positively what actions you will be doing once this goal is achieved and by when you would like to reach this goal. Test to see if your goal is fully clarified by asking yourself, "How will I know when this goal is accomplished?" Write your clarified goal below.

(?)   Can you give me an example of a clarified goal? ▶ Yes! Consider the following examples:

- Instead of, "Pay off debts, and get a job," the clarified goal might be, "By August 1st, secure employment that uses my gift of teaching and my computer science skills as well as provides an average standard of living and $X for monthly debt reduction."
- Instead of, "Stop being critical," the clarified goal might be, "Develop the habit of intentionally saying thanks for specific things throughout my day—so much so that when faced with a tough situation, my first thought is one of thanks rather than criticism or negativity. I want to develop this habit by November 23rd."

Valuing Your Goal

Consider your clarified goal from the previous topic. What makes this goal important to you?

How would reaching this goal benefit others? How would reaching this goal benefit His Kingdom?

Benefit others

Benefit Kingdom

In what ways will achieving this goal help you to experience revitalized health and wholeness and thus reach a dynamic renewal?

How would reaching this goal help you to further fulfill your life's calling(s)?

CORE TOPIC

Remembering the wider and deeper importance of your goal is a vital source of motivation, the fire in the belly that resists the quenching of doubt and distraction.

appraise

For meeting

  4

Determining action steps is like channeling a river: What previously was meandering and murky becomes focused and energetic.

Determining Action Steps

What specific action steps could you take to make progress toward reaching this goal? Ask Him for wisdom and brainstorm as many options as possible.

(?) **What are some examples of specific action steps?** ▶ For instance, using the scenarios from the topic, "Clarifying Your Goal" on p. 180, some specific action steps may include the following:

Securing employment and reducing debt scenario
- Talk to Dave about openings at the school
- Attend job fair in July
- Search online job boards every morning for fifteen minutes
- Research average cost of living in my new city

Developing habit of thankfulness scenario
- Set an alarm on my phone to remind me in the afternoon and evening to write down three items of thanks
- Ask my three closest friends to say, "What are you thankful for in this?" each time they hear me start being critical and negative

Review your responses on p. 179 to the final question in the topic, "Imagining Application," and glean any additional potential specific action steps that would help you to reach your goal. Add these ideas to the list you just brainstormed.

Next, review your list of brainstormed options, and mark the ones you think would most effectively help you to reach your goal, taking into account your values (p. 126) and priorities (p. 97).

Finally, of these marked action steps that you think would be most effective, use the space below to list which ones you plan to do and by when you would need to complete each to reach your overall goal.

strategize

(?) **What if my marked action steps include smaller steps?** ▶ If the action steps you just listed include multiple smaller steps, list these specific smaller steps, and note by when you would like to complete each one in order to reach your overall goal. For instance, if the specific action step is to attend a job fair in July, smaller action steps could include the following:

- Update résumé by June 1st, and ask Sue to proof it by June 15th.
- Buy résumé paper, and print twenty copies by June 20th.
- Research standard interview questions, and prepare responses by June 26th.

For meeting

 3 4

CORE TOPIC

Preparing to succeed is like getting ready to run a 10K race: You trade your clumsy house slippers for sleek running shoes, you let your support team know where to be to cheer you on and hand you supplies, you study the course map to see where the water stops are, and you mentally prepare to complete the course. In short, you remove the obstacles that would trip you up and utilize the resources that will help you cross the finish line.

Preparing to Succeed

Consider your specific action steps from the previous question. On a scale of one to ten (with ten being, "I am looking forward to doing this!" and one being, "I am dreading this!"), how enthused are you about each of these action steps?

If your answers were not at least an eight for each of your specific action steps, what would increase them to an eight, nine, or even to a ten?

What challenges might you encounter as you take these action steps? What will most help you overcome these challenges?

In what ways might your mindset need to change in order for you to effectively take these action steps and reach your goal? What words of Truth would be helpful to remember in making this mindset change?

Which of your strengths, gifts, skills, and habits will aid you in completing your action steps to reach your goal? How will each specifically aid you?

What support from others would you find helpful? How will you go about seeking this support?

How will you celebrate once you reach your goal?

? **Is this process of applying insights practically as outlined in this focus area good to use with other aspirations that I have?** ▶ Yes! In fact, one primary way of reaching a dynamic renewal is through continually discerning ways to apply your most significant insights so that they may benefit yourself and others. And so, if this process (or parts of it) has been helpful for you in discerning practical application of insights through clarifying a specific goal, then— as you have energy, motivation, margin, and His leading—use the process outlined in this focus area to work toward any additional aspirations or goals you may have.

A Focus on Culmination

Final Encapsulation

Imagine encapsulating the entire season of life that you have been addressing during this *Returning Well* journey, including the full meaning of it, in a single sketch. Describe or sketch it on the following page that has been intentionally left blank for this purpose.

→

CORE TOPIC

A final encapsulation sketch is like a stunning panoramic view taken from the summit of your Returning Well journey. Words alone can rarely do it justice.

For meeting

 2 3 4 **5** 6

What is most significant to you about this final encapsulation?

What do you think is the significance of this encapsulation to the Kingdom?

How could this sketch aid you in communicating your cross-cultural life, experiences, and insights with others?

Reaching a Dynamic Renewal

A **dynamic renewal** is experiencing revitalized health (physical, mental, emotional, spiritual, relational, and vocational) and wholeness during the season of life following a transition. It is achieved by engaging the process of skillfully implementing action steps (that have been discerned from honing and applying debriefing insights) in such a way as to benefit others and self.

Given this definition of renewal, use the following pages to consider in what ways the process of renewal in each of the specific areas has already begun in your life and what will help the process of renewal to continue.

→

CORE TOPIC

Reaching a dynamic renewal is like springing up new shoots of vibrant life out of a severed stump: Life may not look the same as it did before, but there is vitality, there is beauty, and there is revitalized health and wholeness. And there is thriving...

For meeting

  4 **5** 6

assess

In what ways has the process of renewal already begun for you in the following areas of your life?	What will help this process of renewal to continue for you in the following areas of your life?
Physical	
Mental	
Emotional	

In what ways has the process of renewal already begun for you in the following areas of your life?	What will help this process of renewal to continue for you in the following areas of your life?
Spiritual	
Relational	
Vocational	
	→

What else, if anything, would assist you in reaching a place of renewal?

CORE TOPIC

Questions & Insights

Glean and Go Forward

Once you have completed this chapter to your satisfaction, take a moment to identify which items you would like to focus on with your companion. Star them or jot them to the left.

CHAPTER TWENTY-TWO

Crafting Your Communications

Let's not lose heart in doing good.
In due season, we will reap a harvest if we do not become faint.

Be steadfast, immovable, abounding in the work of Him always,
knowing that your toil is not worthless in Him.

Upon re-entry, most cross-cultural sojourners face the daunting task of communicating their cross-cultural life, experiences, and insights to those in their primary culture. What makes this task so daunting? Unique communication styles, diverse cultural etiquette cues, distinct repertoires of experience, differences in vocabulary, varying expectations, as well as the emotional disruption that re-entry often provides are just a few of the reasons. But, despite the complexity, such a task is not an impossible feat. Following are some ideas to make crafting your communications a doable, and maybe even an enjoyable, endeavor.

Embrace the Significance of Your Entrustment

You have likely been entrusted with valuable wisdom and extraordinary experiences that others have not. And your thoughtful testimony to these may just be what is used to encourage others to live with increasing compassion, love, humility, admiration, dedication, and wisdom. Embrace the significance of this entrustment by humbly and carefully crafting your communications in such a way as to honor Him, further His Kingdom, and bring about a greater good. As you do, you can trust that your labor is not in vain.

Before You Consider Your Words, Compassionately Consider Your Listeners

Which aspects of "Crafting Your Communications" were most helpful for you?

"Putting myself in my listener's shoes and realizing that maybe it isn't because they don't care after all."

Although potentially not obvious, your listeners may have internal obstacles that impede effective communication. On the outside, it could seem that they don't care, when, in fact, something else might be going on. Before you consider your words, compassionately consider your listeners and the obstacles to communication they may be encountering:

- Some people you encounter may feel so ignorant about your work or host culture that they don't even know where to start, so they don't.
- Others may feel guilty or inferior because they, thinking themselves not as devoted, have not traversed over land and sea for their values and calling and thus would rather avoid the subject of your work and subsequent return.
- Some may fear being awkward, causing offense, or feeling stupid. So, they tense around you, say something inappropriate, or avoid you entirely.
- Others may feel pressed for time; thus, they refrain from engaging you in any meaningful conversation despite their genuine interest.
- Still others want to hear your heart, but they have such a difficult time imagining what your life was like. Because of this, when you start sharing they glaze over, almost as if you are speaking a foreign language. If you did language learning, you probably know the feeling!

Knowing the existence of these and other obstacles will help you discern not only what to share but also how to share it. As you converse with others, be alert to the potential presence of these obstacles. Then, as you encounter them, humbly and compassionately craft your communications, both non-verbal and verbal, in such a way as to remove them so that your exchange may be mutually valuable.

To get you started in the process of overcoming communication obstacles, this chapter contains tools and resources for removing them. Watch for this icon in the margin for practical tips on applying these tools and resources as you seek to overcome communication obstacles.

Stabilize Your Sharing with Three Elements

Telling others about your season of life that you lived in your host culture will likely require these three elements:

- a person willing and able to converse,
- available time for a conversation, and
- a place conducive to communication.

Like a footstool with three legs, if one leg is missing, the footstool will topple. Begin to stabilize your sharing by watching for cues that a person is open to conversing with you. Next, be sensitive to your listener's sense of time. Simply asking, "Is this a good time to talk?" or, "How much time do you have?" may save much frustration. Finally, be aware of your environment and its influence on your exchange. If the location is not fitting for a conversation, either find a way to manage, or go someplace else. Taking steps to ensure that these three components exist as you share with others will help you create a stable structure favorable for a beneficial conversation.

When others have genuine interest but are pressed for time, be thankful for their interest, and ask them if there would be a better time or way to converse.

Choose Words That Build Up, Not Tear Down

As you share with others, take timeless wisdom to heart, and only speak words that are good for building others up—according to the needs being presented—so that your words may be a gift of encouragement to those who listen. As you talk with others, ask yourself the following questions:

- What are the needs of those in front of me?
- How can I use my words to build up this person/these people as well as the people or organizations I am talking about?
- How could I craft what I say to encourage my listeners?

When your listener feels fearful and ends up saying inappropriate things, graciously acknowledge their effort, and use their comments as a starting place for sharing.

Further, your listeners will not always ask questions you think are intelligent or say things you find encouraging. Rather than balk, give thanks that they are willing to engage you, and then find a way to use their questions or comments to lead into a productive and uplifting conversation.

Know the Influence of Your Expectations on Communication

Your expectations have influence. When you experience a strong or surprising emotion, consider your expectations by asking yourself these questions:

- How did I think this would go?
- How did I expect them to respond?
- How did I expect myself to respond?
- For what outcomes was I hoping?

Many emotions come from the difference between your expectations and reality. For example, if you anticipate that your family and friends will desire to know about your season of life that you lived in your host culture, yet they neither ask any questions about it nor seem at all interested in things that deeply matter to you, then you will likely experience disappointment. Alternatively, if you don't expect your family and friends to have much time to listen, and instead they not only ask questions but also look at all your pictures, listen to you for as long as you want them

Which aspects of "Crafting Your Communications" were most helpful for you?

"It was a great reminder of how to communicate. Because our host culture and primary culture are so different, it is easy for us to get frustrated. So it's nice to have a practical reminder about how to speak to others about our experience."

to, and help with the logistics of re-entering, then you will likely experience delight. Thus, the discrepancy between reality and your expectations often produces your emotions, both positive and negative.

Being aware that your emotional responses may stem from unmet expectations will help you manage your emotions, particularly your negative ones, by doing what you can to change reality and/or adjust your expectations. This in turn will greatly influence your communication with others. How? Imagine that someone you know is disappointed in you. How would you approach them? You might be reticent to talk, hesitant in your actions, and fearful of disappointing them further. Now, imagine that someone else you know is delighted to see you. How would you approach them? You might greet them with a big smile, share openly, and enjoy an energizing conversation with them.

In the same way, others respond to the emotions they perceive you are communicating. If, because your experiences do not match your expectations, you communicate annoyance, apprehension, disappointment, or boredom, others may be less eager to engage you. But, if instead you keep your expectations in line with your experiences, you will have a better opportunity to communicate joy, gratitude, acceptance, and admiration. This will encourage others to respond warmly to you and thus create the best possible environment for good communication to happen.

Customize Your Conversations Using Six Building Blocks

Conversations will be as varied as there are people. Given that no one-size-fits-all exists, think of each conversation that you have as an opportunity to create a unique structure, and be prepared with several conversational building blocks. Then, as each conversation begins and continues, wisely choose which block would best fit next.

☐ **Building Block One: Listening**

Although it may seem circuitous, in most situations it will behoove you to listen before you speak. As you listen and seek to understand, not only will the person you are listening to likely feel heard and then desire to hear you, but also you will know how to tailor what you share to better suit your listener when the time comes for you to speak. In turn, both of these advantages of listening contribute to creating a mutually edifying exchange. To prepare to listen well, consider the following questions:

How would others know that you are really listening to them? What would they notice about you?

What are your biggest challenges to listening well? What might help you overcome these challenges as you listen to others during this season of re-entry?

What cues indicate to you when it is appropriate to speak instead of listen?

☐ **Building Block Two: The Basics**

Some people will be completely uninformed regarding the life that you lived in your host culture. To the extent that you are able, given confidentiality and security requirements, create a basic-building-block statement that tells them who, what, where, and for how long. For example, "I worked with ABC organization teaching fourth grade students in the northern region of EFG country for just over six years." If they seem interested to hear more, you can choose another building block to continue the conversation. If not, give thanks that one more person knows a little more about your host-culture life as well as what He is doing in other parts of the world.

Write your basic-building-block statement below.

☐ **Building Block Three: Questions to Continue**

Always offer your conversation partner an easy way out of the conversation if he or she gives you cues that they would rather not engage in further conversation. But, if he or she does desire to continue the conversation, have a repertoire of open-ended questions (i.e., questions that cannot be answered with a yes or no response) readily available. Prepare some questions that allow you to further share your life experiences as well as some to draw out your conversation partner. On the following page are some sample questions to consider using as well as to help you brainstorm your own question list.

Which aspects of "Crafting Your Communications" were most helpful for you?

"Remembering to listen to others and not just talk. Remembering that there are appropriate/beneficial times to share, and there are times when it's not the best to talk about your foreign experience (and wise to know the difference)."

Develop a basic-building-block statement as well as natural open-ended questions to engage in conversation with those who feel ignorant.

For meeting

 2 3 4 5 **6**

When sensing guilt or inferiority in another, acknowledge the value of their work and passions by being genuinely interested in what they have to say, by asking open-ended questions, by humbly listening to them, and by highlighting the importance of their contributions.

- What about this cause/country/culture interests you the most?
- How long have you lived in this city?
- How long have you been part of this fellowship/group/organization?
- What do you like about this city/fellowship/group/organization?
- What new developments have there been recently in this city/fellowship/group/organization?
- What is your occupation? What do you enjoy most about it?
- What does a typical day in your life/in the life of your family look like?
- What do you enjoy doing for fun?

Write below several open-ended questions that would feel natural for you to use to encourage a conversation.

Additionally, consider adding to your list the open-ended questions you brainstormed on p. 118.

Which aspects of "Crafting Your Communications" were most helpful for you?

"I think it was how to use stories. The whole guidebook helped me to remember and appreciate stories (events and experiences). Then, it was great to think through how to use them to actually communicate to people from my primary culture."

☐ **Building Block Four: Stories**

Well-told stories magnificently draw people in, impart understanding, and move the heart and mind, often in a disarming way. Develop a repertoire of several stories, preferably of individuals or specific events, that each encapsulates one crucial aspect or one key theme of what He did in or through your cross-cultural work.

Consider at least three potential stories that you could share and ask yourself the following questions:

- What crucial aspect or key theme does each story illustrate?
- What influence do I want each story to have on my listeners, i.e., what do I want them to think, feel, or do as a result of this story?
- What are the most pertinent and significant details of the story?

Use the following pages to consider these questions as they pertain to your three potential stories. If desired, for additional story ideas look back at your responses to the topic, "Faith Encounters," on pp. 104–105.

Potential story	
Crucial aspect or key theme	**Pertinent and significant details**
Desired influence on listeners Thoughts Feelings Actions	

Potential story	
Crucial aspect or key theme	**Pertinent and significant details**
Desired influence on listeners Thoughts Feelings Actions	

For meeting

2 3 4 5 **6**

Potential story

Crucial aspect or key theme	Pertinent and significant details
Desired influence on listeners	
Thoughts	
Feelings	
Actions	

When you see someone glaze over, share a story of a specific event or individual that encapsulates much of the work that you did.

As you review your potential stories, ensure that each one honors Him as well as the persons, organizations, and/or cultures included in the story. Additionally, consider if you need to ask for permission prior to sharing any of your stories.

Next, know how long it takes to tell each of your stories. If a person or group says that they only have a certain amount of time for you to share, honor them and share for that length of time (or less, especially when sharing in Western-culture group settings). If they want to know more, you may continue as time allows and as they show additional interest.

☐ **Building Block Five: Debriefing and Renewal Insights**

The insights that you have found significant as you have journeyed through debriefing to renewal may also prove to be significant to others. Be ready and willing to share these insights, as appropriate, as well as specific examples or stories that show the difference each insight has made or is making in your life. Your personal growth may encourage your listeners in fulfilling their greatest life calling(s) while also helping you re-adjust.

Review your responses from Chapter Twenty-One (pp. 176–190). Which insights would both be beneficial for others to hear and also valuable for you to share?

List them below, including specific examples that demonstrate how each insight has been and/or continues to be valuable in your life.

Beneficial insights	Specific example of each insight's value

What were some of your most poignant take-aways from engaging *Returning Well*?

"Learning how to communicate to others my process of everything that happened and where I am today with it all."

Consider your final encapsulation sketch from p. 186. How might this sketch also help you to communicate these insights to your hearers?

For meeting

□ **Building Block Six: Ideas to Help in Re-Entry**

For those who are genuinely interested in your personal well-being and want to help, be prepared with ways that they can tangibly assist you in re-entry. Below, list some ways that others could practically help you as you re-enter.

In Conclusion,
Anticipate the Value of Crafting Your Communications

Communicating your cross-cultural life, experiences, and insights to those in your primary culture will likely be challenging. It will take time and energy to understand yourself and your listeners. It will take patience and humility to listen first and respond well to ignorant or critical comments. It will take wisdom and love to craft conversations that uplift, encourage, and renew. But such effort is valuable because your labors in communicating may be precisely what our Creator uses to build His Kingdom and accomplish undertakings of great worth and lasting value. The task before you may not be easy, but few things of such tremendous value are.

Which aspects of "Crafting Your Communications" were most helpful for you?

"I loved the sentence 'but such effort is valuable because your labors in communicating may be precisely what our Creator uses to build His Kingdom.' Love that statement! I totally agree! Communication is important, and there is work that goes into it."

Congratulations on completing your journey through Returning Well! I do hope and trust that your debriefing has been effective and your renewal dynamic. I'd love to hear how Returning Well has made a difference in your life. Contact me at: www.ReturningWell.com/contact. Many Blessings!

Resources

Did you know that, among other related resources, the "Serving as a Returning Well Companion" article and the "Cast Away Content Advisory for Faith-Based Audiences" are available at www.ReturningWell.com/Resources or by following the QR code below? They are! Be sure to provide the password, "SERVING" when requested.

Serving as a
Returning Well Companion

If you have been given this article, you are highly trusted and have been asked to play a significant role in the life of your friend (or family member, client, colleague, etc.).[1] Your friend has engaged the re-entry resource *Returning Well: Your Guide to Thriving Back "Home" After Serving Cross-Culturally*. With this resource, your friend has been encouraged to seek out a trusted individual with whom they can effectively debrief their recent season of cross-cultural life in order to reach a place of dynamic renewal.[2] They have chosen you to walk alongside them on this re-entry journey. This article seeks to answer the most critical questions pertinent to your role as a *Returning Well* Companion.

What is Re-Entry?

You are meeting with your friend during **re-entry**, which is the term used to describe the experiences a person has once they return to their **primary culture** (most likely the home culture in which they grew up) after having

lived and adapted to a **host culture** (the foreign culture where they have been living). **Culture**, for the sake of this article, is defined as the habits, customs, and beliefs that characterize a particular social or ethnic group.

When a person enters their new host culture, they often invest themselves in learning the culture and language. They may experience **culture shock,** which is described as a state of distress experienced when a person is bombarded with the newness of foreign customs,

---

[1] The remainder of this article will use "friend" to refer to these roles. Also note that in keeping with a casual style of writing, this article uses the plural "they" and "their" to refer to singular antecedents.

[2] An **effective debriefing** is reflecting on a recent season of life in order to process the specific aspects of it (events, experiences, emotions, decisions, relationships, thoughts, and actions), understand its impact personally and communally, recognize and accept its paradoxes, identify personal growth and things learned, and bring about a meaningful closure. Effective debriefing naturally leads to renewal. A **dynamic renewal** is experiencing revitalized health (physical, mental, emotional, spiritual, relational, and vocational) and wholeness during the season of life following a transition. It is achieved by engaging the process of skillfully implementing action steps (that have been discerned from honing and applying debriefing insights) in such a way as to benefit others and self.

habits, and language. But as they go through the process of adapting, their lifestyle and values change, which over time, changes them.

Once they return to their primary culture, they experience **reverse culture-shock**, also known as **re-entry shock**. Often, this is more difficult than the original culture shock itself. The person expects to be returning to that which is familiar, i.e., their primary culture; however, they soon realize that not only have they changed, but also their "home," including the people, has changed. They may feel like a foreigner again in what was supposed to be their home.

A person going through re-entry may have many different reactions ranging from joy, excitement, hope, acceptance, anticipation, gratitude, and relief, to grief, anger, anxiety,

fear, embarrassment, loneliness, discouragement, disillusionment, resentment, irritability, criticalness, indecisiveness, confusion, and withdrawal. Left unattended, these varied reactions can manifest in physical symptoms such as illness, fatigue, depression, and insomnia. Such experiences are hard enough, but if a person faces judgment and criticism from those in their primary culture for having these reactions and symptoms during re-entry, the difficulty of the transition is only exacerbated.

But despite these challenges of re-entry, it is also a season that holds great potential value. If a person in re-entry is able to effectively process (i.e., journey through a debriefing to renewal) and communicate their cross-cultural life, experiences, and insights, this will significantly contribute to them thriving in the next season. And also, it may be just what their Creator uses to bless His people and further His work in their primary culture and beyond. The *Returning Well* process is specifically designed to unleash this potential value, and you are a significant part of that process.

What's my Role? How Do I Help?

The first way to help your friend in re-entry is to provide **uninterrupted time** for your friend to **confidentially** share their experiences. Each time you meet with your friend for the purpose of debriefing that leads to renewal, allow about two hours for them to share and you to actively listen. If a person feels rushed, it will be difficult for them to explore and share deeply. Further, your friend has been encouraged to meet with you six times over one of the following time periods:

- six weeks (one meeting per week),
- three months (two meetings per month),
- six months (one meeting per month).

Ask your friend what their preferred time period is, and note that a suggested plan for each of these meetings, including specific questions, is provided at the end of this article. Further, commit to never repeat anything shared during this time, and make that commitment known to your friend before you begin. Please don't miss this! Confidentiality is imperative! Finally, only allow those with a personal invitation from your friend to join these meetings. An environment of trust is indispensable for this time to be effective.

Next, give your friend a **grace-filled and patient presence.** Your demeanor of grace and patience can create a place where your friend feels safe to process the myriad emotions and thoughts they are experiencing without fear of a negative response. Show acceptance of strong emotions as well as silence. Simply your presence is a gift that combats one major challenge of re-entry: isolation.

Because your friend's cross-cultural experiences may have been so different than the experiences of others, your friend may be used to seeing people's eyes glaze over when they share their stories. Thus, you can offer **non-glazing empathy,** putting forth the energy necessary to remain engaged as they share. Sincerely seek to understand their story by putting yourself metaphorically in their shoes. Imagine what their life was like, who was important to them, and what was meaningful about their time in their host culture. Attempt to recognize and acknowledge how their season of life lived cross-culturally fits into their life as a whole and how such experiences might be used in their future.

Lastly, you can be a **non-judgmental explorer** who seeks to understand your friend's story by avoiding the following: interrupting, giving advice, and sharing your own stories. Please don't miss this either! It is imperative that you make space for your friend to talk. Consider the time a success if you talk only three percent of the time. Use this three percent to acknowledge what your friend is sharing and ask **open-ended questions** (i.e., questions that can't be answered with a yes or no). While your friend shares, avoid offering suggestions or trying to "fix" your friend or their situation. Further, avoid "why" questions as they often put people on the defensive.

Thank you for taking the time and energy to fully engage this vitally important task. One very consistent theme discovered as others used the preliminary version of this guidebook was the value of a skilled companion. The majority of those with the most successful outcomes from *Returning Well* all had trusted companions that walked alongside them in these ways. And so, as you serve as a companion, you are helping your friend reach a dynamic renewal—this may be the **best re-entry gift** they will ever receive!

What's the Plan?

On the following pages is a suggested plan for the six meetings laid out in *Returning Well* and open-ended questions to consider using at each. Before your first meeting, you are encouraged to watch *Cast Away,* a movie that depicts transition, adjustment, and re-entry. Your friend has also been encouraged to watch it, which will enable the two of you to share a common reference during your meetings. Your friend has a "*Cast Away* Content Advisory for Faith-Based Audiences" should you desire to be aware of scenes that may require viewer discretion. Although watching *Cast Away* is encouraged, doing so is not required to serve as a companion. Finally, also note that you do not need your own copy of *Returning Well* to serve as a companion.

"I thought it [Cast Away] was a tangible example of what one experiences in a new host culture and upon their return to their home culture…not only for those who had the experience, but also as something that could be referenced to help others understand what it's like to re-integrate into a culture/society that others expect you to claim, know, and relate to."

What helped to make the time with your companion(s) successful?

"Them being a listening ear. Not trying to fix or solve my problems but letting me talk and think through things and process things with them."

"Uninterrupted time."

**Meeting One
Focusing on Building
Rapport and Getting
Started**

The goal of this first meeting is to build rapport with your friend and facilitate an intentional conversation that assists them in processing their initial transition experiences. To achieve these goals, use the following questions as starting places for listening well, and be sure to leave time for the wrap-up questions.

Exploration Questions for the Majority of Your Meeting
- What parts of the movie *Cast Away* most resemble your experiences?
- What has re-entry been like for you thus far?
- What do you most desire to tell people about your season of life that you lived in your host culture?
- What questions do you wish people would ask you? *(If appropriate, ask your friend the questions they mention.)*

Optional Exploration Questions
Use the following questions as your friend demonstrates energy and interest.
- Who were the most important people to you?
  ‣ What made these people important to you?
- What do you miss the most from your host culture?
  ‣ What do you miss the least?
- What were some of the most difficult parts about your life in your host culture?
- What joys from your time in your host culture stand out to you?

Wrap-up Questions for the Final Portion of Your Meeting
- What will help make our time together the best it can be for you?
- What do you hope our meetings together will help you to accomplish?
- How else can I be helpful to you during this time?

Consider closing your time together by asking your Creator to bless your friend's Returning Well journey as well as your future meetings together. After this, ask your friend when they would like to meet again.
- When would you like to meet again?

For meeting

Meeting Two, Meeting Three, and Meeting Four
Focusing on Part Two: "Inquiring"

The goal of these meetings is to help your friend effectively process the questions and insights most pertinent to them from the chapters in Part Two: "Inquiring" of *Returning Well*. Before each of these meetings, your friend will engage questions related to their life in their host culture and then discern which questions they would like to further explore or insights they would like to share in their meeting with you. The following questions will help you to assist your friend in effectively processing these things. Again, your role is not to "fix" your friend; your role is to be a non-judgmental explorer and use these questions as starting places for

listening well to your friend as they share and process what is most important to them. And finally, be sure to leave time for the wrap-up questions.

<u>Exploration Questions for the Majority of Your Meeting</u>
- What additional thoughts, if any, did you have from our last meeting?
- Which question or insight would you like to focus on first in our time together?
    - What makes this item meaningful to you?
    - What would you like to process or explore about this item? *(Help your friend process this item by listening well, reflecting back their thoughts to them, and asking open-ended questions. After your friend completes their processing on one question or insight, repeat this pattern, and ask what insight or question they would like to focus on next, what makes it meaningful to them, and what they would like to process regarding that item. When no other insights or questions arise, move to the wrap-up questions.)*

<u>Wrap-up Questions for the Final Portion of Your Meeting</u>
- What was most significant to you from our time together today?
    - What difference do you think that will make for you going forward?
- What requests would you like me to bring before our Creator for you? *(You may be able to ask this question more overtly if you are meeting in a spiritually open environment. Either way, consider closing your time together by bringing these requests before Him.)*
- How else can I be helpful to you during this time?
- When would you like to meet again?

For meetings

"I liked that I had time to reflect and [talk with my Creator regarding] the questions in Returning Well. But, then it was encouraging to talk through the questions with my companion and get a chance to express my discoveries to another person."

What could your companion(s) have done differently to provide a better experience for you?

"Asked more questions. Listened more than talked. Helped me come up with action steps. [Lifted up my requests to our Creator] with me."

What would have made the time with your companion(s) better?

"If we had been more focused in our conversations."

Meeting Five
Focusing on Chapter Twenty and Chapter Twenty-One

In Chapter Twenty, your friend will pull together all of the insights that they have collected during their *Returning Well* journey thus far. Then, in Chapter Twenty-One, they will discern specific ways to apply those insights, including defining a goal and tangible action steps for living out renewal in their next season of life. Your goal is to continue to be a grace-filled and patient presence and to use the provided questions as starting places for listening well as your friend considers critical steps toward renewal. As before, be sure to leave time for the wrap-up questions.

<u>Exploration Questions for the Majority of Your Meeting</u>
- What additional thoughts, if any, did you have from our last meeting?
- What would you like to focus on in our time together?
  - › What makes this item significant to you?
  - › What would you like to explore or process about this item? *(Help your friend process this item by listening well, reflecting back their thoughts to them, and asking open-ended questions. After your friend completes their processing on this first item, repeat this pattern, and ask what they would like to focus on next, what makes it significant to them, and what they would like to explore regarding it. Once no other items arise, consider the optional exploration questions, or move to the wrap-up questions.)*

<u>Optional Exploration Questions</u>
Use the following questions as your friend demonstrates energy and interest.
- As you considered all of the gleanings that you collected in Chapter Twenty, what themes did you see?
  - › What value do these themes hold for you as you move forward?
- To the extent that you feel comfortable sharing, what were your five most significant insights (from p. 177)?
  - › What difference do you expect these will make in your coming season?
- What is the goal that you committed to work toward in Chapter Twenty-One?
  - › How can I be a support to you, if at all, as you take steps toward your goal?
(In this chapter, your friend is also encouraged to draw a sketch that visually represents their season of life that they lived in their host culture, including the meaning of it. The two following questions pertain to that topic.)
- What was your final encapsulation sketch?
  - › What is significant to you about that sketch?

<u>Wrap-up Questions for the Final Portion of Your Meeting</u>
- What awareness do you now have that you did not have before our meeting today?
  - › What is the value of that awareness for you going forward?
- What requests would you like me to bring before our Creator for you?
- How else can I be helpful to you during this time?
- When would you like to meet again?

For meeting

Meeting Six

Focusing on Chapter Twenty-Two and Bringing Closure to Your Time Together

This meeting has two goals. The first is to help your friend process the communication strategies they developed in Chapter Twenty-Two: "Crafting Your Communications." The second goal is to bring about closure to your time together by celebrating key insights and solidifying next steps for living out renewal. To

achieve these goals, use the following questions as starting places for listening well, and be sure to leave time for the wrap-up questions.

Exploration Questions for the Majority of Your Meeting

- What additional thoughts, if any, did you have from our last meeting?
- For this meeting's agenda, we can focus on some questions I have that are specifically designed to help you process Chapter Twenty-Two, or we could focus on something else of importance to you from your *Returning Well* journey. What would you like? *(If your friend chooses to focus on something of importance to them, utilize the exploration questions that you used in Meeting Five. Otherwise, continue to the following questions.)*
- What was most valuable to you from Chapter Twenty-Two?
  - ➤ What makes that valuable to you?
- What is most difficult for you when it comes to communicating about your host-culture life with those in your primary culture?
  - ➤ What is different about the times you are able to communicate well?

(Chapter Twenty-Two encourages your friend to create a statement to use in talking with others that includes basic information about their time in their host culture. The following question pertains to this statement.)

- What is your basic-building-block statement from p. 195?
  - ➤ How comfortable are you with using this statement?
  - ➤ What, if anything, would help make it more natural for you to use?
- What stories and insights that you listed in Chapter Twenty-Two do you hope to share with others?
  - ➤ What influence do you hope these stories and insights will have?

Wrap-up Questions for the Final Portion of Your Meeting

- What do you most want to remember from all of our meetings?
  - ➤ What difference are these items already making in your life?
- What next steps will keep you moving toward a dynamic renewal?
- What requests would you like me to bring before our Creator for you?
- How else can I be helpful to you as you move forward?

For meeting

CAST AWAY CONTENT ADVISORY
FOR FAITH-BASED AUDIENCES

You are encouraged to watch the movie *Cast Away*[1] as part of your *Returning Well* experience. However, note that **viewer discretion is advised**. The following list includes areas of questionable and/or objectionable content in *Cast Away* for faith-based audiences. The chapter references below correspond to the movie chapters. Note that the following descriptions include movie-plot spoilers. Finally, whether you are a cross-cultural sojourner or a companion, note that although you are encouraged to watch *Cast Away*, you do not need to watch the movie for your participation in the *Returning Well* process to be effective and beneficial. The *Returning Well* process is effective in and of itself.

Events / Scenes
- Allusion to Adultery: In Chapter 2 from 00:03:42 to 00:04:11, a husband is pictured with another woman in sleep attire.
- Kissing:
  - In Chapter 4 from 00:13:21 to 00:13:51, Chuck and Kelly kiss as an unmarried couple.
  - In Chapters 28 and 29 at 02:04:36, 02:05:54, and 02:06:35, Chuck and Kelly (who is now married to another man) kiss before parting ways.
- Allusion to Cohabitation: In Chapter 4 from 00:13:57 to 00:14:50, Chuck and Kelly fall asleep (fully clothed) on a couch together.
- Innuendo: In Chapter 4 from 00:16:22 to 00:16:30, a family member says a sexual innuendo during the holiday meal.
- Frightening/Intense: In Chapter 7 at 00:23:20, a plane crashes and passengers are injured.
- Gruesome: In Chapter 13 from 00:46:45 to 00:50:00, Chuck finds and buries the bloated body of his colleague.
- References to Considerations of Suicide:
  - In Chapter 22 at 01:26:49, Chuck retrieves rope from around the neck of a wooden figure.
  - In Chapter 30 at 02:09:10, Chuck tells Stan about his suicide considerations.

Language
- His Name Spoken in Vain:
  - In Chapter 4 at 00:15:31 and 00:16:18, during the holiday meal.
  - In Chapter 5 at 00:19:19, as Kelly and Chuck exchange gifts.
  - In Chapter 22 at 01:29:40, as Chuck contemplates leaving the island and at 01:30:34, as he searches for Wilson.
  - In Chapter 28 at 01:59:03 and 02:00:32, during Chuck and Kelly's conversation.
- Disrespectful/Questionable Language Spoken:
  - In Chapter 21 at 01:21:46, as Chuck wakes up and at 01:24:57, as he makes a rope.
  - In Chapter 22 at 01:29:40, as Chuck kicks Wilson out of the cave.

---

[1] *Cast Away* is the movie where FedEx® employee Chuck Nolan (played by Tom Hanks) adjusts to living a very different life on a deserted island after a plane crash. Visit www.ReturningWell.com for suggestions regarding where to buy or rent *Cast Away*.

Index

About the Author

MELISSA CHAPLIN has spent much of her life asking and relishing questions. Always in search of the perfect question, phrased in just the right way, Melissa is thrilled when she sees a question open a door, spark an insight, or illuminate the way forward.

Fairly early in life, He called her to join Him in His work around the world. After several stints of cross-cultural service, she was anticipating officially launching her career in Asia. However, that is when He asked a question that altered her course: "You said you would go, but would you stay?" Taken aback and a bit humbled, she said yes and began her career in supporting cross-cultural sojourners.

Since that start, she has whole-heartedly poured herself into walking alongside cross-cultural sojourners who are going, staying, leaving, and returning. For over a decade, she has been traveling the world through her feet, her knees, her phone, and Skype—listening to, loving, and serving those who are seeking to love people and cultures that were at one time foreign to them.

Melissa is a devoted follower, wife, mom, learner, educator, and a credentialed life coach through the International Coach Federation. Her heartbeat is to live today in light of eternity, taking practical steps to love and obey Him. One of her great joys is to walk alongside those in re-entry, truly helping them to return well.